PRAISE FOR *MANAGING NONCOMPLIANCE AND DEFIANCE IN THE CLASSROOM*

"This book is an invaluable resource for teachers, behavior specialists, and school teams interested in creating a positive learning environment for students. Geoff Colvin provides practical advice for addressing student noncompliance in ways that are easy to integrate into your classroom, school, and district. Whether you are a teacher interested in improving social and academic outcomes for your students, a behavior specialist, or a behavior team looking for tools and resources to embed within your schoolwide discipline system, this is the book for you!"

Rachel Freeman
Associate Research Professor and Director of the
Kansas Institute for Positive Behavior Support
University of Kansas, Lawrence, KS

"Finally, a book derived from research but written with practical examples so teachers can better understand how to develop successful interventions in addressing noncompliance in the classroom."

Heather Peshak George
Assistant Professor and Co-Director
University of South Florida
Positive Behavior Support Project, Tampa, FL

D1597729

"Dr. Colvin is a true leader in the fields of education and psychology. He effectively presents empirically based strategies for use in proactively managing noncompliance and defiance in the classroom in a straightforward and practical manner. In addition, the research-based strategies in the text are appropriately supplemented by chapter summaries, case studies, and reproducible materials. In short, this book is simply a must have for teachers and school personnel seeking to effectively manage student behavior and improve student achievement in our nation's classrooms today."

R. Anthony Doggett
Associate Professor and Program Coordinator
School of Psychology Programs, Mississippi State University
Mississippi State, MS

"Noncompliance and defiance in the classroom are important issues that face educators today. In this book, Dr. Geoff Colvin provides a helpful 'roadmap' for school teams. The case studies provide real examples that make the information easily understood and translated into real life situations. The book provides practical, easy-to-use, reproducible tools for assessing problem behaviors and developing effective intervention strategies. With the use of these tools, students' on-task behavior can increase, and educators can more efficiently deliver instruction and maximize instructional time. This book is invaluable for school teams addressing noncompliance and defiance in the classroom. It is an excellent resource for creating a positive, safe, and productive learning environment."

Sylvia Martinez and Laura Zeff
District Behavior Specialists
Los Angeles Unified School District, Los Angeles, CA

To my daughter Kylee and son-in-law Sean,
in celebration of their marriage, September 6, 2008.

"To get the full value of joy,
you must have somebody to divide it with" (Mark Twain).

Managing
NONCOMPLIANCE
and DEFIANCE
in the Classroom

A Road Map
for Teachers,
Specialists,
and Behavior
Support Teams

GEOFF COLVIN

Foreword by Randy Sprick

CORWIN
A SAGE Company

For information:

Corwin
A SAGE Company
2455 Teller Road
Thousand Oaks, California 91320
(800) 233-9936
Fax: (800) 417-2466
www.corwinpress.com

SAGE India Pvt. Ltd.
B 1/I 1 Mohan Cooperative Industrial Area
Mathura Road, New Delhi 110 044
India

SAGE Ltd.
1 Oliver's Yard
55 City Road
London EC1Y 1SP
United Kingdom

SAGE Asia-Pacific Pte. Ltd.
33 Pekin Street #02-01
Far East Square
Singapore 048763

Printed in the United States of America

Library of Congress Cataloging-in-Publication Data

Colvin, Geoffrey, 1941-
Managing noncompliance and defiance in the classroom: a road map for teachers, specialists, and behavior support teams/Geoff Colvin; foreword by Randy Sprick.
    p. cm.
Includes bibliographical references and index.
ISBN 978-1-4129-6088-5 (cloth)
ISBN 978-1-4129-6089-2 (pbk.)
    1. Classroom management. 2. School children—Discipline. 3. Problem children—Behavior modification. I. Title.

LB3013.C65 2009
317.102'4—dc22   2008046602

This book is printed on acid-free paper.

09 10 11 12 13 10 9 8 7 6 5 4 3 2 1

Acquisitions Editor:	David Chao
Editorial Assistant:	Brynn Saito
Production Editor:	Jane Haenel
Copy Editor:	Amy Rosenstein
Typesetter:	C&M Digitals (P) Ltd.
Proofreader:	Sue Irwin
Indexer:	Kirsten Kite
Cover and Graphic Designer:	Scott Van Atta

Contents

Insert: *Master Chart for FBA and Intervention Plan:
The Road Map;* **and** *Glossary of Terms for FBA Strategies*

Foreword

Student misbehavior presents one of the biggest barriers to academic achievement facing our schools today. In *Managing Noncompliance and Defiance in the Classroom,* Dr. Geoff Colvin addresses two of the most difficult and frustrating categories of misbehavior encountered by teachers (noncompliance and disruptive behavior) and provides a wealth of strategies for preventing and intervening with these problems.

Noncompliance from a student is the quickest way for an educator to feel totally helpless. When a teacher gives a direction and a student says, "You can't make me," the teacher immediately realizes, "Oh my, the student is right." From this feeling of helplessness, many teachers may fall into a pattern of trying to MAKE the student follow the direction by issuing the demand more loudly or emotionally, or by threats that imply, "You do it or else . . ." Either of these approaches can result in a battle of wills between the student and the teacher wherein the teacher tries harder to MAKE the student comply, while the student tries harder and more publicly to demonstrate that, "YOU CAN'T MAKE ME!" To avoid such power struggles, some teachers may just let the student have his way—that is, the student is allowed to ignore the direction and thus learns he can choose to follow directions or not. Either of these approaches from the teacher (power struggles or just letting the student call the shots) serves to positively reinforce the student's noncompliant behavior—which you will remember from Psych 101 only increases the future occurrence of the noncompliant behavior. In this book, Dr. Colvin provides practical suggestions for avoiding power struggles and actually gaining compliance from the student.

Disruptive behavior from students can be equally frustrating to the busy teacher who is now highly accountable for the academic achievement of *all* students. Imagine a 50-minute instructional period (in either elementary or secondary school) in which one student causes a major disruption five times. How many minutes of instruction have been lost? Minimally five minutes? Now let's imagine there are two such disruptive students in the room. Ten minutes of lost instructional time each day means that 20% of instructional minutes have been wasted. If this pattern continues for the entire year, it would be the equivalent of knocking 36 days off of a 180-day teaching calendar. No classroom can afford that kind of instructional time loss. In this book, the reader will find a wealth of strategies for preventing and intervening with chronic and severely disruptive behavior.

For many years Dr. Colvin and I have shared the notion that good instruction and good behavior management are a "chicken/egg" issue. You cannot have one without the other, and one does not precede or supersede the other. In many cases, practitioners and experts ignore this link and focus so much on improving student behavior that they ignore academic deficits. Dr. Colvin has always reminded the field that behavioral and academic issues are inseparable. There are many strategies mentioned in this book that focus on instruction and ensure that students are making academic progress while working to replace noncompliance and disruptive behavior with more socially and academically productive behavior.

I have known Dr. Colvin both personally and professionally for more than 30 years and can state with confidence that he is uniquely qualified to have developed this resource. As a teacher, building administrator, university professor, and staff developer, he focuses on what school personnel can do to help troubled children be educationally successful. Although his research and writing cover the breadth of behavior issues, from schoolwide prevention to the needs of the most troubled students, he has always been one of the leading experts on dealing with noncompliance, emotional escalation, and severely disruptive behavior, and he is a master at synthesizing research into easy-to-implement practice. Just as an aside, he is also one of the most personable, friendly, and funny individuals one could ever be privileged to spend time with.

In this book, Dr. Colvin first helps the reader develop a deep understanding of the nature of noncompliant behavior and how to assess the nature of the problem. This is somewhat analogous to making sure that a mechanic has an understanding of how internal combustion engines work and how to run some basic diagnostic procedures before beginning to tinker with the mechanism. With basic knowledge and efficient diagnostic tools, the "tinkering" of the mechanic and the educator will be less likely to cause damage and more likely to create efficient and effective plans for solving the presenting problem.

In addition to this base-level information from Part I of the book, Dr. Colvin goes on in Part II to provide a variety of strategies for developing and implementing evidence-based interventions that have a demonstrable track record of success with noncompliant and disruptive behavior. These are not "theoretical" suggestions. They are practical procedures that can be implemented in either general or special education settings in both elementary- and secondary-level classrooms, reflecting one of his major strength's—translating research into "I can do that tomorrow" strategies for the busy educator.

This resource will be useful to individual classroom teachers who wish to upgrade their professional skill in dealing with challenging students. In addition, this book can be of great benefit to specialists and members of problem-solving teams who have responsibility for analyzing problems and designing intervention plans for a student who chronically exhibits noncompliance or severely disruptive behavior. In fact, the book will serve as a great book-study resource for an entire staff to work through collectively.

The practitioner, teacher, or specialist will find this book to be an accessible and user-friendly guide to understanding the function of misbehavior, for efficiently collecting essential information, for analyzing the nature of the problem, and (perhaps most importantly) for developing intervention plans that have a high probability of helping the student learn to function cooperatively, respectfully, and responsibly. This of course has the benefit of making the teacher's life easier, but even more importantly, can create life-altering benefits for the student who exhibits chronically noncompliant or disruptive behavior. What greater gift can an educator give to a student?

Randy Sprick, PhD
Author and Staff Developer
Safe & Civil Schools
Eugene, OR

Acknowledgments

I wish to sincerely acknowledge Zig Englemann for his significant contributions in helping me to understand the nature of noncompliance and the critical relationship between using what is presented to the students and thereby predicting their subsequent behavior. The book we wrote in the early eighties on compliance training, through Zig's insights, helped shape the way I have approached problem behavior and its solutions throughout my career, and especially in this book.

Randy Sprick deserves my special thanks for his early feedback in the framing and focus of this book. Randy has also helped me to translate an idea or a concept into language and concrete procedures that educators can follow and implement with confidence.

I am also grateful to Brion Marquez for his unique contribution, which I hope is reflected in this book. Brion, through our work together in producing a video teacher training program on addressing noncompliance, highlighted the need to communicate in a way that helps teachers clearly see and visualize what you have in mind.

I wish to thank the following friends and colleagues who made contributions and provided helpful feedback to various content areas in this book: Drew Braun, Carl Cole, Celeste Dickey, Kurt Engelmann, Rob Horner, Kent McIntosh, Krista Parent, Tim Rochholz, Jerry Silbert, Scott Spaulding, and George Sugai.

Finally, thanks are due to Tina Wells for her editing work and to Kylee Lee for her assistance with the layout of the manuscript.

■ **PUBLISHER'S ACKNOWLEDGMENTS**

Corwin gratefully acknowledges the contributions of the following individuals:

Rachel Freeman, PhD
Associate Research Professor
Director of the Kansas Institute for Positive Behavior Support
University of Kansas
Lawrence, KS

Heather Peshak George, PhD
Assistant Professor, Co-PI and Co-Director
University of South Florida
Tampa, FL

David Tudor
State Personnel Development Grant Coordinator
Office of Superintendent of Public Instruction
Olympia, WA

About the Author

Geoff Colvin draws on his experience as a classroom teacher, both in special and general education, school administrator, educational consultant, and research associate at the University of Oregon.

He is a nationally recognized educational consultant who has assisted personnel in more than 200 school districts and agencies, nationally and internationally, on the subject of managing problem behavior, teaching challenging students, and school safety planning. He has authored and coauthored more than 80 publications, including the very popular book *Managing the Cycle of Acting-Out Behavior in the Classroom* and the 2000 Telly Award–winning video program "Defusing Anger and Aggression."

As an administrator, he directed a juvenile detention school for five years and was the principal of a countywide school for youth with serious emotional disturbances for five years. He served as the supervisor of special programs with Bethel School District, Eugene, Oregon, for several years, where he still serves as a consultant.

Dr. Colvin has a very special skill in being able to translate theory into practice. He is able to present clear explanations and analyses of learning and behavior and at the same time offer concrete examples with hands-on illustrations. He has a very strong insightful understanding of the relationship between quality instruction and behavior management. His extensive knowledge and experience base, lively speaking style, and keen sense of humor have made him a highly sought-after speaker at national and international conferences.

Presently, he serves as a national educational and behavioral consultant.

Introduction

Educators embrace the teaching profession because they believe they can make a lasting contribution to the lives of young people. Specifically, they make a strong commitment to teach their students skills for life in academic, social, personal, and vocational areas. However, these goals can be seriously challenged when students display disruptive behavior, particularly noncompliance, in the classroom. Moreover, these aspirations can be significantly attenuated if these behaviors occur on a frequent basis.

Noncompliant behavior, such as refusal to follow directions, insubordination, defiance, and oppositional behavior can cause serious disruption to the teaching-learning process in the classroom. These student behaviors significantly interrupt instruction for the teacher, other students, and for the individual student when the teacher has to spend excessive time addressing these problem behaviors. Noncompliant behavior can cause a substantial loss in instructional time and subsequently reduce student learning. In the more serious cases, noncompliant behavior also can impact an administrator's time in following up with the student and possibly with the parents.

In addition, sustained noncompliant behavior, along with other problem behavior, can negatively impact teachers' motivation and longevity in the field. The U.S. Department of Education for years has consistently reported the grim results of high rates of teacher turnover, especially early in their careers. Granted, there are many factors that contribute to this problem, but student disruptive behavior is frequently listed as a major determining factor.

Teachers have ranked noncompliance as one of the most troublesome and challenging behaviors they have to deal with on a regular basis in the classroom. It makes obvious sense that if a student is noncompliant in the classroom, the teacher's ability to teach and the student's ability to learn are seriously restricted. For example, suppose a teacher asks the students to open their books to page 54 and complete the math problems, and one or more students do not follow this direction. The teacher then has to go through a series of procedures to determine the locus of the problem, as there are many reasons why the student may not be following the direction. For example, the student may be sick; may not have heard the direction; may have lost his or her book; may be upset following a nasty incident on the bus ride to school; may have ongoing difficulties with the subject; or may be in a foul mood and will not cooperate. The challenge is for the teacher to quickly assess what may be happening and encourage the student to cooperate with the direction. However, if the teacher misreads the situation, there is likelihood that the student may escalate his or her behavior, which will consume more time and effort from the teacher and disrupt instruction. The complications arising from this apparently simple teacher request of, "Open your books to page 54" make noncompliance a challenging behavior for teachers to address effectively and efficiently.

Although this book is primarily designed to directly address noncompliant behavior in the classroom, there are two very important perspectives that will strongly influence the effectiveness of interventions to change noncompliant behavior. The first perspective is that the schools and districts need to have a strong, concerted, and systematic focus on ensuring that students are successful in school, especially in regards to academic achievement. For students to be successful with their academics, typically, they must cooperate with their teachers and become engaged with instruction in a productive and responsible manner. The second perspective is that schools and school districts need to engage in comprehensive efforts to make their school environments as positive, safe, and welcoming as possible. It is of paramount importance to understand that problem behavior is most effectively targeted when the *whole* school environment supports desirable behavior. In this way, efforts in the classroom to establish expected behaviors such as cooperation, respect, safety, and responsibility are supported on a schoolwide basis.

This book is designed as a resource for teachers, specialists (personnel charged with teacher support especially in the area of problem behavior), and behavior support teams (groups of educators responsible for developing interventions for students who display chronic problem behavior). There are two parts. In Part I the focus is on understanding noncompliant behavior. Chapter 1 addresses the seriousness and pervasiveness of noncompliant behavior and the negative outcomes experienced by students displaying these behaviors both during their school days and in later life. Chapter 2 presents information on how to define noncompliant behavior and how to grasp its various and subtle forms displayed by students in the classroom. This understanding is taken further in Chapter 3, where details of procedures for systematically assessing noncompliant behavior are described. The components of this assessment provide the framework for analyzing noncompliant behavior leading to the development of systematic intervention plans. The overriding assumption is that if the reader has a solid understanding of noncompliant behavior and can gather accurate assessment information, the teacher, specialist, and behavior support team will be in a strong position to develop effective intervention plans.

In Part II, strategies and procedural details are presented for developing and implementing interventions to establish cooperative behavior and to reduce noncompliant behavior. These intervention plans are derived from information obtained from the systematic assessment procedures. In Chapters 4, 5, and 6, several strategies have been selected and described, drawn from research and best practices for each component depicted in the assessment model. Chapter 7 presents information on guidelines for selecting specific strategies in designing an intervention plan. Case studies also are presented to provide illustrations of how the range of noncompliant behavior can be systematically targeted. The final chapter, Chapter 8, brings together the direct link between the functional behavioral assessment (FBA) questions and corresponding pool of strategies for FBA components in a master chart or road map. A glossary of terms for the strategies is also provided for ease of recall for the reader. A separate insert is included at the back of the book linking the FBA questions, bank for strategies, and glossary of terms.

The reader is referred to an appendix section at the back of the book, which contains copies of the forms, checklists, and tables presented throughout the book. These appendices may be reproduced or adapted for personal use in the classroom, school, or district.

PART I

Understanding Noncompliant Behavior

It is quite puzzling to many educators why noncompliant behavior is such a pervasive and troublesome behavior when it appears to be such a straightforward issue. On the surface, noncompliance should be quite simple to understand and manage. Simply put, did the student follow the teacher's direction, yes or no? If yes, reinforce the student. If no, provide a negative consequence. Obviously there has to be more to understanding noncompliance than this seemingly uncomplicated paradigm and subsequently more to managing the behavior in classrooms.

The purpose of this section is to provide an in-depth analysis of noncompliant behavior that addresses the subtle and elusive ramifications of the behavior. Clearly, if the behavior is properly understood, there is more chance for teachers, specialists, and behavior support teams to design effective intervention plans.

There are three chapters in this section. Chapter 1 describes the seriousness and pervasiveness of noncompliant behavior in schools. Factual information is presented on the high prevalence of noncompliant behavior and the worrisome, long-term harmful outcomes for students who display noncompliant behavior. Chapter 2 deals with defining noncompliant behavior with descriptions of various facets of noncompliant behavior likely to be encountered in classrooms. Chapter 3 presents details for developing a systematic procedure for assessing noncompliant behavior. This assessment provides specific information on the factors contributing to and sustaining noncompliant behavior. This assessment procedure provides key information enabling teachers, specialists, and behavior support teams to develop precise and effective intervention plans.

1

Urgency of the Problem

The following comments by educators, regarding the behavior of some students, have been expressed in many different ways over the years:

She just won't mind. Once she gets set on something, that's it, and it is a real battle to get her to do anything else. (Kindergarten teacher)

He just refuses to follow directions when we start formal instruction, and he won't cooperate with any form of group instruction. (Elementary school teacher)

She treats rules like a challenge, then goes out of her way to break them. (Middle school teacher)

He gets very angry when he is asked to make corrections on his assignments and then shuts down and won't do a thing. (High school teacher)

She has an authority problem. Whether it is a school rule or a direction from a teacher, you can almost guarantee she will find a way to be defiant. (School psychologist)

I find students who are sent to me for noncompliance are a difficult group to address. They already have a chip on their shoulder by the time they get to me, and you can tell they are not going to cooperate with what I try to arrange. (School principal)

Each of these comments, from K–12 educators, describes a variety of instances of students not doing what is asked of them. This resistance to requests is typically called noncompliance and is the focus of this book. Educators have identified two major concerns regarding this behavior: (1) the high prevalence of noncompliance in schools, and (2) the harmful outcomes of chronic noncompliant behavior.

PREVALENCE OF ■
NONCOMPLIANCE IN SCHOOLS

Over the past several years, there has been considerable focus on taking steps to ensure that schools are positive, welcoming, and safe environments for learning (Colvin, Kame'enui, & Sugai, 1993; Mayer, 1998; Sprick, Wise, Marcum, Haykim, & Howard, 2005; Sugai & Horner, 2005). Although the emphasis in this trend has been to implement evidence-based, positive, and proactive practices, there is still a need for constructive procedures in managing problem behavior when it arises. It is very evident in research on the kinds of problem behaviors schools face that noncompliance and its analogues (disobedience, defiance, insubordination, and oppositional behavior) are highly prevalent and are of serious concern to educators.

Skiba, Peterson, and Williams (1997) conducted an extensive analysis of office referral data of 19 middle schools serving 11,000 students from a large Midwestern city. These office referrals, numbering 17,045 across the schools, were coded by behaviors warranting an office referral. Results indicated that the most common reason for referrals was noncompliance (27.6%), representing more than double other common reasons, including conduct interference (12.8 %), disrespect (10.7%), and fighting (10.7%), respectively. In an earlier study, Colvin, Kame'enui, and Sugai (1993) found across three schools that noncompliance was either the most common or second most common reason for referrals.

More recently, a review of data from School-Wide Information System, SWIS (May et al., 2003) on reasons for office discipline referrals was conducted from data for an urban school district in Oregon, composed of approximately 5,700 students. Results showed that for the elementary schools, K–5, the highest ranking reasons for referrals were as follows: first, aggression/fighting 28.8%; second, noncompliance/disrespect 27.9%; and third, inappropriate language, 11.3%. In the case of the middle schools, Grades 6–8, by far the most common reason for referrals was noncompliance at 31.0%, with aggression/fighting ranked a distant second at 17.7%. At the high school level, the top three reasons for referral were defiance, 20.8%, cell phone misuse, 15.9%, and fighting, 7.3 %, respectively.

Spaulding and colleagues (2008) reviewed an extensive database of office discipline referrals from SWIS encompassing 1,709 schools from 43 states, Grades 1–12, for the 2005–2006 school year. Their analyses on highest ranking reasons for referral showed the following: Grades 1–5, fighting at 32.4%, defiance at 29%, and inappropriate language at 10.7%. In the middle schools, Grades 6–8, defiance ranked first at 31.2%, with disruption a distant second at 18.2%. For the high schools, Grades 9–12, defiance ranked first at 24.2%, tardiness for class at 24.0%, and truancy at 21.3%.

These studies have indicated that noncompliant behavior in the classroom, for some time now, has been the overall *highest ranking reason for office discipline referrals for Grades 1–12*. It is safe to conclude that noncompliant behavior in the classroom is a highly prevalent ongoing behavior of great concern in schools.

■ HARMFUL OUTCOMES OF CHRONIC NONCOMPLIANT BEHAVIOR

Students who display chronic noncompliant behavior are at risk for a number of serious negative outcomes that can be summarized in terms of (1) damaging life outcomes in general and (2) detrimental effects on academic achievement.

Damaging Life Outcomes

In the early 1980s, Walker and Rankin (1983), as part of an extensive eight-year research project, surveyed a national sample of more than 1,100 teachers, K–12, regarding the expectations general education teachers held for students in their classrooms. The results showed that more than 90% of teachers participating in the survey rated noncompliance and defiance toward teachers as one of the least acceptable maladaptive behaviors in their classrooms.

Similarly, 23 years later, Lane, Wehby, and Cooley (2006) found that (1) following teacher directions still remained a high-priority standard expectation of teachers for their students across grade levels and that (2) failure to meet these expectations resulted in several serious negative outcomes within and beyond school settings, especially regarding academic underachievement and social relationship issues.

Pediatricians and service providers have reported over many years that noncompliance of young children is a recurring serious problem for parents (Bernal, Klinnert, & Schultz, 1980; Kalb & Loeber, 2003). In a longitudinal study of children exhibiting noncompliance, Kochanska, Aksan, and Koenig (1995) found that noncompliance, especially severe noncompliance, is especially stable over time. This means that these students are likely to exhibit noncompliance throughout their school career, at home, and into later life (Walker, Colvin, & Ramsey, 1995).

The prognosis for students who exhibit severe noncompliance at an early age is particularly grim. Researchers have reported for many years the prospects for children who display antisocial behavior, which includes noncompliance, are very serious with outcomes listed in Box 1.1.

BOX 1.1   NEGATIVE OUTCOMES FOR STUDENTS DISPLAYING ANTISOCIAL BEHAVIOR AT AN EARLY AGE

- Peer rejection
- Increases in off-task behavior in lower grades
- Bonding with other antisocial students, including involvement with gangs
- Dropping out of school
- Involvement in juvenile crime and later on adult crime
- Ineffective relationships as adults
- Inability finding and keeping employment
- Serious mental health issues as adolescents and adults

Source: Compiled from Dishion, French, and Patterson, 1995; Eddy, 2001; Walker, Colvin, and Ramsey, 1995.

Detrimental Effects on Academic Achievement

It is logical to assume that most students who display noncompliant behavior on any regular basis will have problems in succeeding with their academic work. The reason is obvious; when teachers provide instruction, they typically require tasks of their students that involve following directions and expectations. Students who do not follow these directions will have difficulty completing the tasks set by the teacher, which will in turn affect their academic achievement. Kauffman (1997) so aptly noted that "low achievement and problem behaviors go hand in hand" (p. 247).

Sutherland, Wehby, and Yoder (2002) reported that academic deficits of students are further exacerbated by the modified instruction they receive, which is brought about by their disruptive classroom behavior. Van Acker, Grant, and Henry (1996) reported that for students with emotional and behavioral disorders, the rates of correct oral responses were approximately 0.84 to 1.2 per hour. In addition, teachers praised these students' correct responding at a rate of 0.68. This means that these students with behavioral issues in the classroom received teacher praise for correct responding at a rate of *only four to five times per day*. In addition, these researchers reported that teacher responses were five times higher for correct compliance responses to teacher directions than for correct responses to academic tasks. Several other studies reported that students who exhibit problem behavior in the classroom have low academic achievement scores compared with their peers, who by and large cooperate in the classroom (Carr & Punzo, 1993; Colvin, 2004; Cotton, 2000; Gunter & Conroy, 1998).

In effect, there is a clear correlation between academic underachievement and problem behavior. A cyclical relationship exists between the impact of problem behavior in the classroom and the kind of instruction that is delivered to students who display noncompliant and disruptive behavior.

CHAPTER SUMMARY   ■

Ample documentation shows that noncompliant behavior in classrooms and schools has been a long-standing behavior of concern. For many years, it has been one of the most common reasons, if not the most common reason, for office referrals and is listed high on teacher reports as a demanding behavioral challenge. Noncompliant behavior not only causes classroom disruption but can also have many negative effects throughout the student's life in school, at home, and in the community. It is imperative for educators and service providers to take urgent measures to more fully understand the nature of noncompliance and to take more effective steps to change this very challenging, pervasive, and disturbing behavior.

2

Defining Noncompliant Behavior

One of the main reasons noncompliance is such a problem behavior in classrooms is that it is not clearly understood, or it is oversimplified and not given sufficient depth of analysis and response the behavior warrants (Walker & Walker, 1991). The purpose of this chapter is to provide teachers, specialists, and behavioral support teams with a full description of the nature of noncompliance. Special emphasis will be placed on providing a framework for understanding the many nuances of noncompliant behavior in the classroom.

The following areas are addressed: (1) necessary conditions for noncompliant behavior, (2) common synonyms, (3) model for defining noncompliance, and (4) variations of noncompliant behavior.

■ NECESSARY CONDITIONS FOR NONCOMPLIANT BEHAVIOR

Before student behavior can be labeled noncompliance, certain conditions must be met. If these conditions are not met, the behavior should not be called noncompliance. This does not mean that the behavior is not a problem. Rather, it means that strategies for addressing noncompliant behavior may not be appropriate for addressing this behavior. Conversely, if the following conditions are in place, the definition, assessment, and strategies may then be applied.

School Authority

For a student to exhibit noncompliant behavior, a direction must be given by *a school authority*. A person in authority refers to any member of the faculty, including administrators, certified and classified staff, substitute teachers, and, in some cases, sanctioned volunteers.

Some students are prone to treat staff members differently. For example, a teacher may ask a student from another classroom to pick up the trash he or she threw on floor in the hallway, and the student replies, "You are not my teacher." Similarly, it is well known that students are more likely to follow directions from the principal versus a noon-duty assistant. Often, students will be more compliant with the classroom teacher compared with the classroom educational assistant. It is also well known that students often treat substitute teachers with less respect and cooperation than their regular teachers. The faculty needs to work hard, in a coordinated manner, to communicate to their students that they are expected to follow directions and cooperate with *any authorized adult* in the school building regardless of the adult's position.

Explicit and Implicit Directions

Compliance or noncompliance refers to whether or not students have followed directions presented by a school authority. The directions may be *explicit* or *implicit*. An explicit direction is unambiguous in its interpretation and directly delivered by school personnel. For example, the teacher may present a direction to the class, "Open your math book to page 54, please." There is no question as to what book and page is needed and what the students are expected to do. Or, the teacher says, "Great discussion. Thank you. Now, I want each of you to write at least a page on the key events that lead to the Civil War and turn it into me at the end of this class session." In this direction, a number of tasks are required of the students. They are to take a page, begin writing on the events leading to the Civil War, and turn in their page at the end of this particular class. Each of these directions is explicit.

Other directions are implicit. These usually include established routines, expectations, and rules in the classroom and school. For example, the teacher may say, "Listen everyone, it is time for PE." The directions implied in this announcement are for the students to follow the routine of putting their materials away, clearing their desk, pushing in their chair, and lining up at the door. In the hallways, there is the expectation (implicit direction) that the students are to keep moving to their next class, keep their hands and feet to themselves, walk and talk quietly, and to be seated by the time the next bell rings. In these cases of implicit directions, it is understood that the routines, rules, or expectations have been taught and established so that the students and staff know exactly what is required.

Understanding the Directions

It is particularly important when considering issues with noncompliance that the students clearly understand directions and know what is required of them. In an eye-opening study, Shores, Gunter, and Jack (1993) reported that less than 20% of teacher directives to students, with and without disabilities, were preceded with information that would enable the students to respond correctly. Obviously, students' response to directions cannot be assessed as compliant or noncompliant if they did not properly understand the directions.

Moreover, the language used in the directions needs to be age appropriate and specific enough that the tasks required of the students are clear.

Capacity to Complete the Direction

It is also important for the teacher to have a solid basis of knowing if the direction or task required is something the student is capable of completing satisfactorily. The student must have the necessary skills to complete the task before a judgment can be made on whether or not the student is being noncompliant. If the student does not understand what is required or does not have the skills to complete the task, then further instructional assistance is needed. If the student can complete the task but will not, then there is a basis for assessing the behavior as being noncompliant. This issue is central to understanding the effects of noncompliance, which will be addressed more fully in Chapter 3.

Delivery Tone

An important aspect in presenting directions is the manner in which the teacher delivers the directions. In some cases, students may be disturbed by the way the teacher is presenting directions. For example, they may sense a tone of sarcasm, anger, disrespect, or intimidation. In these situations, the student may react inappropriately to the way the direction is given. The analysis in this case is not a compliance issue, but rather a negative or retaliatory response to the teacher. Teachers should present directions to the students in a calm and respectful manner.

Securing Students' Attention

Another critical issue in presenting directions is the need for the teacher to secure the students' attention prior to delivering a direction. If the students are attending to something else, such as conversations with other classmates, or if they are engaged in a highly preferred activity or perhaps distracted over some private issue, then it will be difficult for them to attend to the direction. In these situations, teachers typically use two steps in presenting directions: first, to disengage the students from what they are currently attending to, and second, to present the direction. For example, a teacher might say, "Everyone, please listen [Step 1: Disengaging the students]. It is time to finish up and turn in your work to the assignment basket [Step 2: Presenting the direction]."

■ COMMON SYNONYMS

In this book, noncompliance is used to describe those behaviors related to following directions and cooperating with school and classroom expectations. Several other terms or expressions are used in schools, service agencies, and the literature to describe the same resistant behavior, including the following:

- Oppositional behavior
- Insubordination
- Refusal to follow directions
- Resistance to directions
- Noncooperative behavior
- Defiance
- Limit testing
- Willfulness
- Stubbornness
- Nonconforming

MODEL FOR DEFINING NONCOMPLIANCE ■

The model for defining noncompliance contains two parts. The first part involves a direction or request given to students from the school authority figure. The second part refers to the response made by the student to this direction. If the student fulfills the request to a reasonable standard, then the response is called compliance or cooperation. However, if the student does not fulfill the request to a reasonable standard, the response is called noncompliance. Figure 2.1, Defining Compliance and Noncompliance, depicts a direction presented to the student and the student options for completing the direction satisfactorily or not. Satisfactory completion of the direction is called compliance or cooperation, while unsatisfactory completion of the direction is called noncompliance.

Figure 2.1   Defining Compliance and Noncompliance

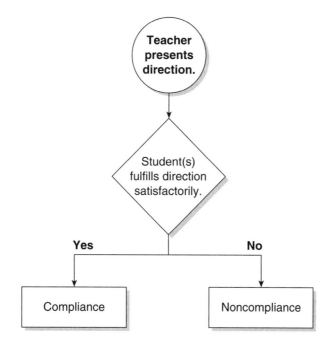

Fulfilling the Direction Satisfactorily

Central to understanding noncompliant behavior in this model is the clause, *student fulfills the direction satisfactorily.* It is probably in this area of clarifying exactly what is meant by "satisfactorily" that makes noncompliance such an elusive problem behavior to address. What does it mean to complete the direction to a reasonable standard or criterion? It is possible for a student to fulfill the direction, but the standard was not satisfactory. For example, the teacher asks a student to sit down. The student continues to visit with another student, then walks halfway around the room, talks to another student, reads an item on the bulletin board, and several seconds later sits down. This response would be called noncompliance because, even though the student did ultimately sit down, an inordinate amount of time was taken to do so. The direction was not fulfilled *satisfactorily.*

■ VARIATIONS OF NONCOMPLIANT BEHAVIORS

A number of common variations of noncompliant behavior center on whether or not a direction has been completed satisfactorily. By learning to understand these nuances of noncompliance, a key focus in this chapter, educators will be in a stronger position to analyze the behavior and develop intervention plans.

Latency

Latency refers to the amount of time elapsing from when a direction is given to the *beginnings* of a response from the student. For example, the teacher says to the class, "Open your math books to page 54, please." A few seconds later, all of the students except one take their books and open to page 54. Meanwhile, one student is tapping a pencil on the desk, looking around, and talking to others. The teacher acknowledges the class for being ready and repeats the direction to the student to have his or her book opened at page 54. The student promptly replies, "I'm getting there. Give me a chance." This response would be called noncompliant because the student took far too long to begin to follow the direction. Part of the criterion for fulfilling a direction satisfactorily involves latency, which is the time it takes for a student to *begin to respond*.

Task Completion Time

Task completion time is the *total* time taken for a student to complete a given direction or task. Suppose the teacher gives a direction that may take several seconds for the class to complete. However, a particular student may string this task out by including several off-task behaviors, thereby taking far longer than the rest of the class to complete the original direction. For example, the teacher asks the class to take a sheet of paper from their notebook, date it, and put their name on it. The class proceeds to follow this direction and waits for the next direction. One student, however, burrows in his desk; fiddles with a mechanical pencil; looks at a magazine; and comments to another student. In the meantime, the rest of the class is ready; the teacher begins to explain the lesson and repeats the direction to the student who is not ready. The student replies, "That's what I am doing. Give me a chance." Presuming the student is capable of doing what the rest of the class was able to do in getting ready for the lesson, this student's response would be determined as noncompliant as the direction was not completed in a reasonable amount of time.

Substandard Response

In this instance of noncompliance, the student completed the task significantly below the standard of his or her capability. For example, the teacher asks the students to complete a page of writing on the discussion subject the Bay of Pigs. One student, a competent student, writes just half a page. Similarly, the teacher directs the class to copy down a paragraph in their very best writing. One student, whose penmanship is above average, writes sideways on the paper in a barely legible manner. In each of these examples, the students produce substandard responses. In one sense, they have responded to the direction given but not to the standard within their ability. In other words, the requests were not fulfilled satisfactorily, which, by definition, is noncompliance.

Granted there could be other reasons for the substandard performance, such as the student is not feeling well or is having a bad day for some reason. These other explanations need to be ruled out before the response can be called noncompliance. To determine that the response is noncompliant, the teacher needs to be reasonably sure that the student is *deliberately underperforming*. Otherwise it is better to give the student the benefit of the doubt and proceed with instruction.

Competing Reinforcers

This variation comes into play when a student is quite engaged in an activity and is directed to proceed to another activity that is less engaging or reinforcing. For example, the student may be playing a game on a computer and is directed to finish up and get ready for math. Some students may resist this direction because they find the computer game much more reinforcing than the math lesson. Or, students may be involved in a fun game at recess, and the bell rings to end recess. Some students may want to continue the game because it is more fun than lining up for class.

In general, noncompliance, or resistance to following directions, may occur in transition times, especially when the current activity is more enjoyable to the student than the next one. Consequently, some students may not cooperate with the teacher's directions to transition to the next activity. Although this lack of cooperation is deemed to be noncompliance, it is important for teachers to recognize that there is an issue of competing reinforcers at play. Consequently, additional steps are usually needed to help the student make these kinds of transitions successfully.

Given there are many forms of noncompliance that may be operating in a classroom, the teacher needs to pinpoint exactly why the student's response can be identified as noncompliance. By understanding and recognizing the various nuances, the teacher is in a sound position to implement strategies described in Part II for developing intervention plans.

■ CHAPTER SUMMARY

It has been well documented that noncompliant behavior is a very challenging behavior for teachers to address effectively. One reason for this situation is that a number of conditions need to be satisfied before the behavior can be called noncompliance. Problem behavior may occur, and if the conditions for noncompliance are not met, then the teacher may incorrectly identify the behavior as noncompliance, which may lead to an ineffective intervention plan and further problems.

It is particularly important for the teacher, specialist, and behavior support team members to have a clear grasp of an adequate definition of noncompliant behavior. A key element in the definition described in this chapter is that the directions given need to be fulfilled *satisfactorily*. The term "satisfactorily" refers to the standard set for an acceptable response. The best guidelines for determining whether a response is satisfactory or not include the following: (1) set a standard based on the performance of the majority of the class, and (2) ensure the student has the ability to make the response at the level of the rest of the class. Once a standard for an acceptable response has been established, the teacher is in a better position to identify the variations of noncompliance that students may exhibit and to develop effective intervention plans accordingly.

3

Systematically Assessing Noncompliant Behavior

Problem behaviors in the classroom can be the bane of a teacher's life. These behaviors can disrupt instruction, cause unrest and tension among students, drain the teacher's energy, and take considerable attention and time to address. It is not uncommon for educators to ask questions like, "What do you do when a student is continually disrespectful in class?" Or, "What is a good strategy for students who do not follow directions on a regular basis?" Or, "I have tried everything to keep this student on task. Do you have any new ideas?" These questions have one point in common. They all ask for a specific strategy to address a persistent problem behavior. Teachers are asking for a "silver bullet" that is likely to fix the problem and fix it quickly. Although it is possible that a strategy could be identified to reduce the problem behavior, the teacher, most likely, will not know why the strategy worked or how the strategy can be adapted as necessary to address other problem behavior. Moreover, if the strategy was effective in reducing a problem behavior, the teacher may apply the same strategy to other problem behaviors and find that it did not work or may have made the situation worse.

The root problem with this approach is that is goes straight from problem to solution. There is *no assessment*, that is, there is no attempt to identify explanations for the problem behaviors. For example, some students may not follow directions because they do not have the prerequisite skills to complete the task. Other students may not follow directions because they were engaged in another activity and did not attend to the directions. A third group of students may not follow the directions because they do not like what they are asked to do, so when they show noncompliance and defiance they may be successful in being removed from the situation. In each of these three cases, the students were not following directions. However, there were very different reasons why the students did not follow the directions, which imply different strategies for addressing each situation. In this first case, the students did not have the skills to complete the task, which suggests that the students need to receive more teaching on the skills or need to be provided with tasks that are at their skill level. The second group did not hear the directions, so the remedy would be to clearly secure their attention first before the direction is delivered. The final group of students wanted to escape from the activity they did not like. Although each of these cases resulted in students not following directions, the explanations were different, which suggested different strategies. It is the assessment, the efforts to explain why the students may not be following the directions, that dictates the kinds of strategies used to address the problem behavior of not following directions. Table 3.1, Assessment of Problem Behavior and Implied Strategies, shows how the assessment of the problem behavior is the link between problem behavior and effective strategies for these three scenarios.

Table 3.1   Assessment of Problem Behavior and Implied Strategies

Problem Behavior "Not following directions"	Assessment	Strategies
Group 1	Lack of skills necessary to complete task	Focus on teaching skills or adapt tasks
Group 2	Not attending or attending to something else	Ensure attention is secured before direction is given
Group 3	Students want to avoid the class activity	Ensure the students are able to perform the tasks required in the activity and perhaps address motivational factors

In general, problem behavior can have many forms and different explanations, which imply different strategies for addressing the problem behavior. To pinpoint these differences in a systematic way, a *functional behavioral assessment* (FBA) approach will be described as follows: (1) an FBA model, (2) description of FBA components, (3) FBA summary and intervention plan, (4) FBA checklist for noncompliance, (5) sources for FBA information and case studies, and (6) additional FBA resources.

A FUNCTIONAL BEHAVIORAL ASSESSMENT MODEL ■

At the heart of an FBA is the gathering of information on *all factors* that may contribute to the problem behavior. Some of these factors may be immediate, such as the students are asked to get ready for a quiz and one student refuses to get ready, acts out, and is then removed from class. The quiz sets the occasion for the noncompliant behavior, and by being removed from class the student is successful in avoiding the quiz. In addition, there may be some history factors, such as the student may have failed a quiz earlier and was punished by his or her parents, or the student knows that failure in the quiz is inevitable because he or she has not done the work to prepare for the quiz. Consequently, quizzes serve as aversive stimulus for the student. All of these factors—the quiz itself, the removal from class, the experience of punishment from parents, and failure to prepare for the quiz—may contribute to the student's noncompliant behavior.

The approach in this book is to systematically identify all the factors that *may contribute* to the problem behavior. With this knowledge, educators are in a strong position to develop an effective intervention plan to reduce the problem behavior and to replace the behavior with one that is acceptable. This process of identifying all the contributing factors has typically been called an FBA. The assumption is that each of the identified components of the assessment plays a role in explaining the problem behavior and must be considered in developing an effective plan to change the problem behavior and establish acceptable behavior.

The goal in conducting an FBA is to gather precise information that will enable a comprehensive intervention plan to be developed to reduce or eliminate the occurrences of these problem behaviors and replace them with acceptable behavior. In this way, the problems are effectively managed, and instruction can be delivered without significant interruption.

Factors Must Be Testable

It is absolutely essential in the process of conducting an FBA and developing a comprehensive intervention plan to *identify factors that can be tested or manipulated*. For example, Gary is always late for school, and the parent indicates he watches TV till early hours in the morning on most nights. It is very likely staying up so late, and subsequent loss of sleep, is a factor contributing to the student's tardiness for the first class. This factor can be readily tested by setting limits on how long the TV may be used at night so the student gets more sleep, making it more likely he will get to school on time. This factor is testable.

By contrast, the parent may report that he has a bad attitude and that is why he is late for school. A bad attitude, although descriptive, is something that cannot be directly manipulated or tested and cannot be used as an intervention. This factor, as such, is not testable.

■ COMPONENTS OF A FUNCTIONAL BEHAVIORAL ASSESSMENT

The behavioral assessment process is typically set in motion by concern over problem behavior exhibited by a student. Educators have the twofold goal of reducing or eliminating this problem behavior and replacing it with an expected behavior. In this book, the goal is to reduce student non-compliance and establish cooperation. The tools for changing this problem behavior are generated from information obtained by reviewing events preceding the student behavior and events following the behavior. The dynamic interaction between these events, FBA, is depicted in a model, Figure 3.1.

This model consists of an interacting cycle involving *four components:*

1. Setting Events

2. Immediate Triggers

3. Problem Behavior

4. Effects of Problem Behavior

The sequence of events or pathway is assumed to be, based on the chronology, that Setting Events precede the Immediate Triggers, which give rise to the Problem Behavior resulting in certain outcomes called Effects of Problem Behavior.

The model is referred to as a *cycle* because the fourth component, Effects of Problem Behavior, usually serves to reinforce the problem behavior and strengthen the whole pathway, so that when the Setting Events or Immediate Triggers recur, there is likelihood that the problem behaviors will be exhibited again. This cyclic nature of the model is represented in the diagram by the arrows connecting the last component, Effects of Problem Behavior, to the Immediate Triggers and to the Setting Events.

Note: The approach in this book is to emphasize the two components that occur before the onset of the problem behavior, Setting Events and Immediate Triggers. The assumption is these components are antecedents,

Figure 3.1   Model for Cycle of Functional Behavioral Assessment

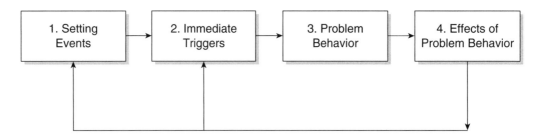

and if addressed effectively, the problem behavior may be pre-empted and not occur. The goal regarding the third component, Problem Behavior, is to reduce or eliminate the problem behavior and replace it with an acceptable behavior. In the case of the fourth component, Effects of Problem Behavior, the intent is to provide outcomes that reinforce the expected behavior and reduce the problem behavior.

DESCRIPTION OF FUNCTIONAL ■ BEHAVIORAL ASSESSMENT COMPONENTS

Each of the four components will be described followed by an application of the model to a noncompliant situation in a classroom.

Component 1: Setting Events

Setting Events refer to the first component in the diagram and include earlier events or continuing events that may set the stage for the problem behavior to occur. Setting Events differ from the next component, Immediate Triggers, in their proximity to the occurrence of the problem behavior. Setting events may have occurred the day before or much earlier, or in a different context to where the problem behavior occurs. For example, a setting event may involve a student who had a serious confrontation at home and was not able to complete the homework assignment. The next day in class, the student was still upset over the conflict at home and the fact that the homework was not completed. When the teacher asked for the homework, the student refused to turn in his notebook, became argumentative, threw books on the floor, and was ultimately removed from the classroom. In this case, the student's serious confrontation at home and failure to complete homework served as *setting events.* The effect of these events carried over to the classroom the next day, leading to noncompliant and disruptive behavior.

Setting Events usually fall into five categories: (1) physiological factors such as health issues (migraines, earaches, sleep deprivation, and illnesses); (2) ongoing conflicts (altercations with family, hostilities with staff or other students, and emotional factors involving relationships); (3) history of failure, such as inability to perform the task or embarrassment from previous unsuccessful attempts; (4) cumulative problems where a series of issues or setbacks build up for the student; and (5) physical issues such as the classroom being too crowded, noise level too high, or the room temperature too hot or too cold.

Component 2: Immediate Triggers

This component refers to the actual context or particular events where or when the behavior occurs. The events or factors may be *concurrent,* which refers to the context of when the problem behavior occurs, such as a spelling quiz, quiet reading time, or bus travel. Or the events may be *antecedent*, occurring just prior to the incidence of the problem behavior, such as the student may be called a name, refused permission to leave the room, or asked to follow a direction (these events are often called *triggering antecedents*).

It is particularly important to identify all events that occur prior to and during the problem behavior. In some cases, the Immediate Triggers are obvious, and plans can be made readily. In other cases, the role of an event may not be obvious and may need to be addressed at a later time, especially if the plan is not working.

Once the Immediate Triggers have been noted, plans can be made to (1) develop measures to enable the student(s) to manage the triggers to prevent occurrences of the problem behavior, and (2) permit the teacher to make adjustments to the context so that the student is assisted in making appropriate responses.

Note: It is often a challenge to see precise differences between setting events and immediate triggers. Immediate triggers, as the name suggests, *set off the behavior*. Setting events *set the occasion for the behavior*. For example, a setting event could be that the student has a severe migraine going into class. The migraine puts the student on edge. When the teacher tells the student that time is running out and that he or she needs to get ready for the next activity, the student reacts and does not comply. In this case, the migraine functions as the setting event, and the teacher direction to get ready serves as the immediate trigger.

Component 3: Problem Behavior

In this component, the behavior of the student, or students, which causes problems in the classroom, is identified. These behaviors include refusing to follow directions, running away, acting out with shouting and throwing materials around, arguing with the teacher, refusal to participate in the classroom activity, altercations with other students, and various aspects of acting-out behavior. The behaviors can be rated as low level, which interrupt instruction to a small extent, such as two or three students engaging in side talk while the teacher is explaining something. The teacher may or may not interrupt the explanation to address these students to secure their attention. The behavior can also be more serious, such as a student who refuses to come to class and is running up and down the hallway banging on doors. In this case, the teacher has to stop instruction to address this student, and it may be quite some time before instruction can resume. Typically the student problem behavior is described in terms of observable features regarding what the student actually does and says.

Component 4: Effects of Problem Behavior

In this final component, Effects of Problem Behavior, the assumption is that problem behavior serves a *purpose*, or *multiple purposes*, for the student exhibiting the behaviors. Some critical questions to ask are, "What does the student gain or avoid from this behavior?" "What happens as a result of the behavior?" "What changes occur either short term or long term when the behavior occurs?" In general, by exhibiting the problem behavior, something changes in the particular setting that serves the student in some predictable way.

Perhaps the simplest and most comprehensive way to look at the Effects of Problem Behavior is to use the long-standing framework of positive and negative reinforcement. Positive reinforcement refers to those effects where the student *obtains* something that is desirable or preferred following the behavior. For example, the student who steals an object gains something he or she wants for free. Another student who talks out in class secures the attention of the teacher. By obtaining something desirable, the student is reinforced and is more likely to exhibit the same behavior again to obtain these outcomes.

Negative reinforcement, on the other hand, is defined in terms of the effects where something aversive or undesirable *is removed* from the student. For example, Sarah does not like to read out loud because she stumbles a lot on many words and is embarrassed. So when it is time for oral reading, Sarah begins to act out and is sent to a time-out area in the corner of the room. By being sent to time-out, Sarah is successful in not having to embarrass herself by having to read out loud.

It is important to understand that in each case the problem behavior may be reinforced. In the first case, positive reinforcement, the student gains something preferred as a result of the behavior. In the second case, negative reinforcement, the student removes or escapes something that is aversive or not preferred.

The term *function of the behavior* is often used in the literature to describe this component in an FBA. However, in this book the word *effect* is preferred because each component in the process serves a particular function, and, consequently, the whole process involving four components serves an important function.

When the fourth component is completed, Effects of Problem Behavior, the *cycle* is likely to resume if the same or similar setting events or immediate triggers occur. The functions of the behavior serve to *reinforce* the whole chain, making it very likely that the problem behavior will persist.

Information obtained related to each of these four components of an FBA, Setting Events, Immediate Triggers, Problem Behavior, and Effects of Problem Behavior, provide the basis for developing a systematic intervention plan for reducing the problem behavior and for developing acceptable replacement behaviors.

FUNCTIONAL BEHAVIORAL ASSESSMENT SUMMARY AND INTERVENTION PLAN

Once the FBA information has been collected, the next step is to summarize and organize these data. For this purpose, an FBA form is recommended. A blank sample form is presented in Appendix A: FBA Summary and Intervention Plan. This form will be used for the remainder of this book. The form is divided into two parts. The first part, upper portion, is the FBA Summary, where relevant data for each of the respective components of the FBA (Setting Events, Immediate Triggers, Problem Behavior, and Effects of Problem Behavior) are listed. The second part, lower portion, is devoted to the details of an Intervention Plan derived from the FBA Summary. Specific strategies are entered in the columns of the chart for the corresponding components of the FBA. At this juncture, only the first part of the form, Functional Behavioral Assessment, FBA Summary, will be completed. The second part of the form, the corresponding strategies, will be addressed in Part II, Chapters 4–8.

Case Study 1

The FBA model will be applied to the following case study presented in Box 3.1 to illustrate the four components of an FBA approach. This narrative is then summarized in Table 3.2, FBA Summary and Intervention Plan, Case Study 1.

Note: This case study will be completed in Chapter 7, where an intervention plan will be generated based on this FBA information.

BOX 3.1   NONCOMPLIANT BEHAVIOR CASE STUDY 1

Bill has often announced how much he hates math. This particular morning, just as the math period was underway, Bill was not following the teacher's directions. He refused to open his math book or get out his notebook and was just sitting there. The teacher gave him a reminder to get started. He said he hates math and folded his arms. The teacher approached him and told him that he could ask for help if he needs it, otherwise he is expected to get out his materials and to start work. Bill replies, "Why bother, it is all a waste of time." The teacher explained to him that if he didn't get ready for math he would have to do it at recess. He then pushed the math book on the floor and said he is not going to do any (expletive) math. The teacher sent him to the office for noncompliance and disrespect.

■ FUNCTIONAL BEHAVIORAL ASSESSMENT CHECKLIST FOR NONCOMPLIANCE

The questions presented in the checklist for noncompliance in Table 3.3 are designed to serve as guidelines for obtaining the FBA information. Responses to these questions are usually obtained from direct observations; FBA interviews with teachers, parents, and the student as appropriate; and a review of school records. Questions have been listed for each component of the FBA. This form also appears as Appendix B and, like other appendices, is reproducible.

■ SOURCES OF FUNCTIONAL BEHAVIORAL ASSESSMENT INFORMATION AND CASE STUDIES

A critical key to developing an effective intervention plan for changing problem behavior begins with gathering *precise* functional assessment information. This information provides possible explanations for the

Table 3.2   FBA Summary and Intervention Plan, Case Study 1 (See Appendix A: FBA Summary and Intervention Plan)

Functional Behavioral Assessment Summary		
Setting Events	Immediate Triggers	Problem Behavior	Effects of Problem Behavior
• Aversion for math (perhaps due to history of lack of success or failure with math) • Issues with anger management	• The beginning of math period • Teacher directions to get materials ready • Engagement with the teacher • The warning that he would miss recess if he didn't get ready	• Refusal to follow the teacher's directions • Maintains refusal to start • Using bad language • Disrespect	• The teacher was drawn into the problem by student's refusal to follow directions • The student was sent to the office, thereby escaping from the math class • Class was disrupted

Intervention Plan		
Setting Events	Immediate Triggers	Increasing Expected Behavior	Decreasing Problem Behavior

Table 3:3 FBA Checklist for Noncompliance (See Appendix B: FBA Checklist for Noncompliance)

Functional Behavioral Assessment Summary

Setting Events	Immediate Triggers	Problem Behavior	Effects of Problem Behavior

• Has the student experienced setbacks with demand before, such as:
  ○ Failure
  ○ Embarrassment or ridicule
  ○ Rejection
  ○ Injury
  ○ Punishment
  ○ Other
• What basis is there to know if the student can perform the task satisfactorily?
• Have there been previous attempts to address the noncompliance?
• Are there nonclassroom-based risk factors such as:
  ○ Home issues
  ○ Hunger
  ○ Substance abuse
  ○ Inadequate sleep
  ○ Transportation to school problems
  ○ Peer conflicts
  ○ Other
	• What is the task or demand required?
	• What words are used by staff in presenting the demand?
	• What are the prerequisite skills for the task?
	• Does the involved student have the prerequisite skills to complete the task?
	• Has the student been on task prior to this demand situation?
	• Other?
		• What does the student do to noncomply?
		• What language does the student use when noncomplying?
		• How does the student avoid the demand or task?
		• How does the student escape the demand or task?
		• How does the student not fulfill the task to a reasonable standard?
		• What do the other students do in this context that is acceptable?
		• Other?
			• What changes occur in setting when the noncompliance occurs?
			• What does the teacher do immediately following the noncompliance?
			• What does the teacher say following noncompliance?
			• What consequences are delivered?
			• What do other students do/say when the noncompliance occurs?
			• Are other adults brought into the picture?
			• Does instruction or the activity stop?
			• Other?

Intervention Plan

Setting Events	Immediate Triggers	Increasing Expected Behavior	Decreasing Problem Behavior

problem behavior, which in turn gives educators direction on what can be targeted and manipulated to change the behavior. These sources provide information on responses to the checklist questions raised for the noncompliance FBA (Appendix B: FBA Checklist for Noncompliance).

Three methods are typically used to gather FBA information: (1) direct observation, (2) FBA interviews, and (3) review of records. These sources can be used to provide responses to the suggested questions presented in Appendix B.

Direct Observation

This source of information involves a person recording the events for a designated period of time, as they unfold in the actual setting where the problem behavior is likely to occur (such as a classroom, hallways, playground, or gymnasium). Researchers typically consider information from direct observations to be more reliable than written or verbal reports from others. Essentially, observations are based on what is directly seen when the behavior occurs versus reports that are based on perceptions or secondhand information (Alberto & Troutman, 2003; Algozzine & Konrad, 2005; Sugai & Tindal, 1995). In addition, the direct observation information can capture the role of interactions between the student and the teacher. For example, the teacher's immediate response to a student's refusal to follow directions may trigger a more serious behavior from the student. Interactions are important information that can lead to specific strategies. For example, an aggressive response from the teacher may lead to student escalation, whereas a calmer response from the teacher may defuse the situation.

Three major limitations exist in using direct observations. First, the information is limited to what is seen and recorded at that particular time. Oftentimes an observer hears comments such as, "You should have been here earlier. Then you would have seen the real thing." In effect, a direct observation functions like a snapshot in time. This problem can be circumvented, to some extent, by trying to pinpoint the problem settings beforehand. For example, the observer could ask the teacher questions such as, "When is this problem behavior most likely to occur?" "When did you last see the problem?" "Can you predict when or where the problem behaviors happen?"

Second, the observer may function as an intrusion or distraction. Just having an additional adult in the room, taking notes and sitting in the corner, may change the dynamics of the classroom. Some students are less likely to exhibit problem behavior if they sense they are being watched. To prevent this problem, the observer could spend additional time in the classroom before the observation is conducted so students get used to the person being in the room. Also, the observer may serve as a helper, moving around the room, checking student's work, and encouraging on-task behavior. The students would then see the observer as an assistant. Such an arrangement would need preapproval by the teacher.

Finally, the observer needs to be carefully trained in recording procedures to ensure that the information is reliable and that observer bias is controlled as best as possible.

The ABC Form

This instrument is a well-established and simple direct observation procedure for recording events associated with problem behavior.

The instrument, ABC, stands for antecedents, behavior, and consequences, respectively. In this book, the corresponding terms are Immediate Triggers, Problem Behavior, and Effects of Problem Behavior. Typically, the form consists of demographic information at the top (such as name of student, teacher, time of day, period, grade) and four columns denoted by Notes, Antecedents, Behavior, and Consequences, respectively. The first column, Notes, serves as a prompt to follow up on any entry that may serve as a Setting Event. For example, the student may mutter, "I am too tired to do any of this." This statement would be noted and may be worth following up to check if the student has inadequate sleep patterns; that is, inadequate sleep could function as a *setting event.* The order of the columns, Notes, Antecedents, Behavior, and Consequences, is consistent with the pathway of the FBA model used in this book (see Figure 3.1 and Appendix A).

A useful function of an ABC Direct Observation procedure is that it can be used to track and analyze interactions, especially between the teacher and the student. Specifically, the student may exhibit inappropriate behavior to which the teacher responds. The teacher's response often serves as an antecedent for the student's next behavior. For example, a student may call out in class (B–Behavior) and the teacher provides a verbal correction that you must raise your hand if you wish to speak (C–Consequence). The student may react to the correction and shout out more. The correction by the teacher served as an antecedent for the student's behavior of shouting out more. For these successive interactions, the usual practice is to enter a "c" in the Antecedents column. The "c" represents the previous consequence serving as an antecedent for the student's next behavior.

A blank ABC form is included in Appendix C.

Using the ABC Form

There are four main steps in completing an observation:

1. Complete the demographic information at the top of the form, including the observation start time.

2. Begin the observation by recording the student behavior (B column) and then quickly record the antecedents (A) and consequences (C).

3. Enter the letter "c" in the Antecedents column when the entry in the consequence column serves as an antecedent for the student's next behavior.

4. Make entries in the Notes column for any additional events or items that may need some follow-up.

Continue these steps until sufficient observation data have been recorded.

Case Study 2

A sample ABC form is presented in Table 3.4 displaying the results of an observation of a student who exhibited noncompliant behavior at the beginning of reading period following recess. It may be necessary to conduct more than one observation to obtain additional information or to verify information obtained from this first observation. It is also desirable to share the ABC information with the teacher to clarify the results as well. This FBA information for Case Study 2 is later used to develop an intervention plan in Chapter 7.

Once the direct observation has been conducted, the next step is for the person conducting the direct observation, usually a specialist or member of the behavior support team, to summarize and organize the information for each component within the FBA format. The results of this observation are presented in Table 3.5, FBA Summary and Intervention Plan, Case Study 2.

Functional Behavioral Assessment Interviews

A second source of information for an FBA comes from FBA interviews. Depending on the circumstances and need, interviews are typically conducted with the teacher and also can be conducted with parents and the individual student as appropriate.

As distinct from the direct observation, interviews can be designed to gather information over a longer period of time. The biggest limitation regarding interviews is that the information is second hand and is restricted to the person's ability to recall detail. In some cases, the teacher's perceptions may be negatively biased because the teacher may be burned out if the problem behavior has been particularly intrusive and has been resistant to interventions over a long period of time.

In general it is best to conduct interviews in conjunction with and prior to direct observations. In this way the observation times can be scheduled based on when the problem behaviors may occur and a connection has already been made with the teacher.

Typically a specialist or someone who is trained in the procedures conducts the interview. In some cases the teacher may self-administer the interview questions.

It is necessary to have specific questions ready for the teacher to respond to when you sit down for the interview, such as the questions listed earlier in Table 3.3, FBA Checklist for Noncompliance. These questions are designed to provide detailed information related to the four components of a functional behavioral assessment: Problem Behavior, Immediate Triggers, Setting Events, and Effects of Problem Behavior.

In addition, it is important to gather information on interventions that have already been tried with the student and to gauge the teacher's impressions on how successful these interventions have been, and under what circumstances they have been successful. It is also helpful to have some questions ready that address positive aspects of the student's behavior. By starting with these questions, the interview may be more positive overall and may lead to more effective interventions.

Table 3.4   ABC Direct Observation, Case Study 2

Student Name: Conrad O'Neill   **Observation Date:** March 23, 2008

Observer: Tabitha Mahoney   **Begin Time:** 9.45 a.m.   **End Time:** 10.00 a.m.

Activity: Reading Instruction   **Class Period:** Reading

Notes (Potential Setting Events)	Antecedents (Immediate Triggers)	Behavior (Problem Behavior)	Consequences (Effects of Problem Behavior)
Check reading grades and check mastery of prerequisite skills for this lesson	Students come in from recess Teacher directs class to open reading books	Sits with arms folded, not opening reading book, tapping his fingers	Teacher acknowledges class for following directions and repeats direction to Conrad
Two other students also were not ready with their reading books	c	Frowns, shuffles feet	Teacher begins reading, approaches him, and whispers to get his reading book out
	c	Stands up and walks around the room	Teacher reads a little more. Tells class to read next page silently and approaches Conrad
	c	Walks away from the teacher	Teacher reminds him to get started or he will have to do his reading during the break
Other two students have their reading book out but are watching the teacher and Conrad	c	Begins to pull material from the bulletin board	Teacher acknowledges class for reading and approaches Conrad, telling him that he has the choice of starting his reading or he will be sent to time-out area
	c	Rushes to the back of the room shouting	He is sent to the time-out area Disrupts class Student escapes reading

Table 3.5 FBA Summary and Intervention Plan, Case Study 2 (See Appendix A: FBA Summary and Intervention Plan)

Functional Behavioral Assessment Summary

Setting Events	Immediate Triggers	Problem Behavior	Effects of Problem Behavior
• Signs of agitation after recess, perhaps social issues at recess	• Teacher direction to open reading book • Teacher's personal direction and close proximity • Teacher raises penalty to begin reading or be sent to time-out area	• Sits with arms folded, not following direction and tapping fingers • Frowns and shuffles his feet • Stands, leaves desk, and walks away from teacher • Rushes to the back of the room and is shouting	• Student off task • Gets teacher to repeat direction • Draws teacher over • Gets personal direction • Maintains off-task behavior • Disrupts some students • Draws threat from teacher to follow directions or miss break • Sent to time-out area • Disrupts class • Escapes from reading class

Intervention Plan

Setting Events	Immediate Triggers	Increasing Expected Behavior	Decreasing Problem Behavior

Conducting a Teacher Interview

When a specialist is assigned to conduct the interview, it is very important for this person to understand that no one in the school situation knows the student who is having behavioral issues better than the teacher (*Note:* In some cases, a paraprofessional may have the best first-hand knowledge of a student). Therefore, to gather sound information, develop, and implement an effective intervention plan, it is very important to carefully arrange and conduct the interview. The following procedural steps are recommended:

1. Arrange a time to meet with the teacher when there is the least chance of interruptions. Inform the teacher beforehand how long the meeting will last—usually 20–30 minutes. Sometimes it is helpful to give the teacher a copy of the interview questions beforehand so the teacher may be less threatened by being "interviewed" and may have a chance to collect some thoughts for the questions. Some specialists prefer to use the word "meeting" versus "interview" as it sounds less threatening. For the same reason, the term "survey" is often used instead of "interview" to communicate a less imposing situation.

2. At the beginning of the meeting, gratefully acknowledge the time the teacher is making available.

3. Avoid being presumptuous that you can readily fix the problem. Rather, communicate that you wish to work with the teacher and others as appropriate to work together in developing a plan.

4. Communicate, as far as possible, that the new plan will try to build on, or accommodate, what has already been tried with some success.

5. Clarify that the information gathered in this interview will also be tied in with other information obtained from direct observations and archival data review as appropriate. In addition, once all relevant information has been collected, a comprehensive plan will be developed with the teacher and other stakeholders as necessary.

6. Explain the format of the interview: Essentially, specific questions will be asked, and the responses will be written down. The questions are usually drawn from the checklist, Table 3.3. The information will then be summarized in an FBA format.

7. Reassure the teacher that the information is confidential and that the original form and notes will not be distributed to anyone. All that will be distributed will be the summary along with summaries from the direct observation and archival data review.

8. Proceed with the interview.

Interview Form

A blank reproducible interview form, Appendix D: FBA Interview Form, is included in the Appendices. Teachers and specialists are encouraged to adapt the form to suit their own needs for gathering the specific information they need for conducting an accurate FBA and developing a useful intervention plan.

Case Study 3

The results of a teacher interview are presented in Table 3.6 showing the teacher's responses to questions related to a student who had a history of noncompliance, especially in the context of transitions. This interview information was then summarized in Table 3.7, FBA Summary and Intervention Plan, Case Study 3.

Review of Records

School records are a permanent product of standard information on students that are kept on file usually at the school or district office. Information usually recorded include grades, attendance, office discipline referrals, transfer records, special education information, medical records, and involvement with other agencies, such as mental health and youth services (Tobin, 2005).

In reviewing student records, educators can obtain a broad-based profile of a student and can identify factors that may contribute to the problem behavior in the classroom. Records also provide a picture of the student's activities and results over a number of years. Records also provide a measure of the depth or gravity of the student's needs and concerns. For example, one student may have received failing grades and a few office referrals, but nothing else is out of the ordinary. In this case, an intervention plan would be developed to support the student's academics and address behavior in the classroom and school. Another student may have failing grades and office discipline referrals and, in addition, have attendance problems, issues at home, and have some involvement with youth services. This student would need a much more comprehensive intervention plan targeting school, home, and the community. A plan involving wraparound services might be advisable for this student (see Chapter 5, Setting Events). In effect the school records can provide information on the extent to which setting events or risk factors may be contributing to the problem behavior.

Although school records are an important source of information for the teacher, specialist, and behavior support team in developing an FBA, there are a number of important considerations that should be addressed (Tobin, 2006). The following guidelines and understandings are recommended in reviewing student records:

1. Become familiar with the laws and policies regarding the use of confidential records, particularly the Family Educational Rights and Privacy Act (FERPA, http://www.ed.gov/policy/gen/guid/fpco/ferpa/index.html).

2. Realize that there is considerable variability in the paper trail for school records. Some information is noted very informally, such as a handwritten note on a piece of scratch paper, while other data are systematically entered in a computer program.

Table 3.6   FBA Interview, Case Study 3 (See Appendix D: FBA Interview Form)

Teacher's Name: Sheila N.   **Date:** March 23, 2008

Interviewer: Marcel Tanner   **Begin Time:** 10:00 a.m.   **End Time:** 10.20 a.m.

Student Name: Emily H.   **Grade:** Fourth

FBA Information

	Transitions
Problem Behavior: Noncompliance	
What does the student do to noncomply?	She keeps engaged on the computer and refuses to finish up and go to science.
What language does the student use when noncomplying?	She just ignores me. Sometimes she stalls and says, "In a minute."
How does the student avoid the demand or task?	Just keeps playing and ignores me.
How does the student escape the demand or task?	Keeps working on the computer, delaying her start on science.
How does the student not fulfill the task to a reasonable standard?	She drags her computer time out as long as she can.
What do the other students do in this context that is acceptable?	They end the break and move to their desks for science in a reasonable time. She can escalate if you push her to move or threaten her with no break next time—she gets angry and belligerent and argumentative.
Other?	
Immediate Triggers	
What is the specific task that is required of the students when the noncompliance occurs?	Finish the break—stop working on the computer.
What words are used by staff in presenting the demand?	I just tell them that in a few seconds we need to switch to science, then I tell them that it is science time.
What are the prerequisite skills for the task?	Understand the directions and do what is asked.
Does the involved student have the prerequisite skills to complete the task?	She knows what has to be done and can do it if she wants to.
Has the student been on task prior to this demand situation?	Yes—it is just she enjoys the computer time more than science.
Other?	

Setting Events	Transitions
Has the student experienced anything aversive with this demand situation before, such as: • Failure • Embarrassment or ridicule • Rejection • Injury • Punishment • Other	Her grades are average. I expect she can do better—it is motivation I think. No, I don't see any of this applying.
Is there a basis to know that the student can perform the task correctly?	Not an issue—it is her choice really to make the transition or not.
Have there been previous attempts to address the noncompliance?	Yes—she seems to have trouble letting go of preferred activities.
Are there nonclassroom-based factors that put the student in a negative frame of mind such as: • Home issues • Hunger • Substance abuse • Inadequate sleep • Transportation to school problems • Peer conflicts • Other	No—perhaps she doesn't have access to computers or games at home so she hangs on at school. I don't know though.
Other?	
Effects of the Noncompliant Behavior	
What changes occur in the setting where the noncompliance is occurring?	Well she gets my attention and time, which prevents me from getting science underway.
What does the teacher do immediately following the noncompliance?	I try to get the class focused on science, then I go back to her to prompt her to finish up.
What does the teacher say following noncompliance?	I follow a usual routine of praising students who transition quickly and remind her to do the same.

(Continued)

Table 3.6 (Continued)

FBA Information (Continued)	
What consequences are delivered?	At this stage I just try to be more positive to the other students.
	If she refuses for long I tell her she will miss recess, or if she gets noisy and belligerent I send her to the Office.
What do other students do/say when the noncompliance occurs?	They just wait. They have seen it before with her when she wants to do her thing.
Are other adults brought into the picture?	Only if she won't go to the office if it gets that far—which happened once.
Does instruction or the activity stop?	Yes. The start of science is delayed, and we wait until she comes to science (sometimes we have started without her—but that's what she wants).
Other?	
Additional Information	
Data	
What classroom data do you have on the student's noncompliance?	She exhibits this refusal to transition about once every other week.
Are there office referral data?	I believe she has had about 1–2 referrals per term.
What are the student's grades?	Average, but I believe she can do better.
Strategies Used	
What strategies have you tried to address the problem?	Incentives for making transition quickly.
	I had her on a contract once and less break time when she didn't cooperate.
What strategies have had some success?	None really.
What strategies may have escalated the student?	Following through on her noncompliance, making her miss the next break or denial of computer time.
Strengths and Reinforcers	
What subjects are strengths?	She likes reading.
What activities engage the student?	Break time with computers and games.
What are the reinforcers for the student?	Extra time on the computer and games with friends.

Table 3.7   FBA Summary and Intervention Plan, Case Study 3 (See Appendix A: FBA Summary and Intervention Plan)

Functional Behavioral Assessment Summary

Setting Events	Immediate Triggers	Problem Behavior	Effects of Problem Behavior
• Grades are average • Question of access to computer use and preferred activities at home	• Teacher announces break time is ending and gives direction to switch to science • Additional prompts from teacher • Follows through with threat of losing next break • Sent to office	• Refuses to switch from computer to science class (transition) • Ignores teacher and uses stalling tactics • Continues on computer, refusing to go to science class • Becomes angry, belligerent, argumentative, and disruptive • Refusal to go to office (once)	• Maintains time on computer • Draws teacher over, engages teacher • Delays the start of science class • Gets out of science • Makes us wait • Misses break time next time (may be sent to office) • Draws in another adult • Delays start of class • Misses science class

Intervention Plan

Setting Events	Immediate Triggers	Increasing Expected Behavior	Decreasing Problem Behavior

3. Note that the information, especially office discipline referrals, can have reliability and accuracy issues. For example, some referrals may be written in "the heat of the moment" where anger or frustration may color the report, whereas if the referral was written later, a different account may have been reported.

4. Be aware that the records may not be current or that there are gaps in the records, requiring considerable time to find the needed information.

5. It is most important to use school record information in conjunction with other sources of data such as direct observations and teacher interviews.

Record reviews are typically conducted in cases where the student has exhibited noncompliant behavior at a chronic level. Generally, record reviews provide a detailed history of the student's noncompliance over time, along with other transgressions at the school level. In addition, the records can provide important information related to setting events such as school performance and risk factors related to school, home, and the community. A record review checklist is presented in Table 3.8 (Appendix E: Record Review Checklist).

Additional Functional Behavioral Assessment Resources

Over the past few years, several excellent functional assessment procedures have been published to guide educators in gathering FBA information in a systematic, reliable, and valid manner. The reader is referred to Box 3.2, Resources for Conducting Functional Assessments, for some recommended resources on the subject of FBAs and interventions.

BOX 3.2   RESOURCES FOR CONDUCTING FUNCTIONAL ASSESSMENTS

Carr, J., & Wilder, D. A. (2004). *Functional assessment and intervention: A guide to understanding behavior* (2nd ed.). Homewood, IL: High Tide Press.

Chandler, L. K., & Dahlquist, C. M. (2005). *Functional assessment: Strategies to prevent and remediate challenging behavior in school settings.* Upper Saddle River, NJ: Prentice-Hall/Pearson Education.

Cipani, E., & Schock, K. (2007). *Functional behavioral assessment, diagnosis, and treatment: A complete system for education and mental health settings.* New York: Springer Publishing Company.

Nelson, J. R., Roberts, M. L., & Smith, D. (1998). *Conducting functional behavioral assessment: A practical guide.* Longmont, CO: Sopris West.

O'Neill, R. E., Horner, R. H., Albin, R. W., Storey, K., Sprague, J., & Newton, J. S. (1997). *Functional assessment and program development for problem behavior: A practical handbook* (2nd ed.). Pacific Grove, CA: Brooks/Cole.

Sugai, G., Horner, R. H., & Gresham, F. M. (2002). Behaviorally effective school environments. In M. Shinn, H. M. Walker, & M. Stoner (Eds.), *Interventions for academic and behavior problems II: Preventive and remedial approaches* (pp. 315–350). Bethesda, MD: NASP Publications.

Table 3.8   Record Review Checklist (See Appendix E: Record Review Checklist)

Student Name:	**Grade:**
Reviewer's Name:	**Review Date:**

Office Referrals

Noncompliance

☐ Frequency
☐ Location
☐ Faculty
☐ Subject
☐ Period of time
☐ History
☐ Other

Other Office Referrals

☐ Skipping class
☐ Fighting
☐ Bullying, harassment, hazing
☐ Other

School Performance

☐ Grades
☐ Participation in school events
☐ Attendance
☐ Peer group relationships
☐ Faculty relationships
☐ Other

Risk Factors

☐ Possession of illegal weapons
☐ Vandalism at school, home community
☐ Transiency
☐ Gang activity
☐ Truancy
☐ School suspensions or expulsions
☐ Court adjudicated
☐ Parents withdrawing student from school
☐ Child abuse
☐ Poverty
☐ Other

■ CHAPTER SUMMARY

Noncompliant behavior in classrooms has been well documented as a common, troublesome behavior for teachers. It has proven to be an elusive behavior to address and change. One reason for this challenge is that the behaviors can look quite similar in the way they are manifested. There are not too many ways in which a student may show refusal to follow directions, test limits, or challenge teachers through defiance. However, there are many reasons or explanations for *why* students exhibit noncompliance. Teachers and specialists must find precise information on why students exhibit noncompliance and why they continue to exhibit this problem behavior.

The key to finding accurate information on explanations of noncompliance lies in the systematic use of FBA procedures. In this chapter, a model for understanding FBA was described in terms of four interacting and cyclical components: Setting Events, Immediate Triggers, Problem Behavior, and Effects of Problem Behavior. Information on each of these components is typically derived from three sources: direct observation, FBA interviews, and review of school records. A summary chart was presented to organize this information within the pathway of Setting Events, Immediate Triggers, Problem Behavior, and Effects of Problem Behavior. Once the FBA data has been derived and summarized, educators are in strong positions to develop a focused and comprehensive intervention plan to change the noncompliant behavior and establish cooperative behavior (discussed more fully in Part II).

PART II

Designing Intervention Plans for Noncompliant Behavior

When the question arises, "What should we do when a student is noncompliant?" the best answer is, "It depends." It was noted that there are many forms of noncompliance that need to be identified before an effective intervention plan can be developed. In addition, a major point made in Chapter 3 is that there are several factors that may be contributing to noncompliant behavior. The functional behavioral assessment (FBA) procedure is designed to pinpoint these factors in the areas of *Setting Events, Immediate Triggers,* and *Effects of Problem Behavior.* Once the FBA information has been completed, the stage is set for developing a reasonably precise intervention plan.

There is a substantial base in published literature from research and best practices describing many effective strategies for targeting factors identified in the components of an FBA. Several of these strategies are compiled and grouped according to the assessment components and are briefly described in Chapter 4, Immediate Triggers; Chapter 5, Setting Events; and Chapter 6, Effects of Noncompliant Behavior. The reader will notice some of the strategies listed are very common classroom practices. If additional strategies are included in an intervention plan for individual students, the standard practices still need to be maintained for the benefit of the other students and also for the purpose of helping to sustain behavioral changes with the target student.

It is important to understand that the strategies included are not meant to be exhaustive. Rather, they are intended to represent a reasonable compilation of established evidence-based practices. Teachers, specialists, and behavior support team members are strongly encouraged to add strategies that they have found to be useful to these lists. However, it should be noted that these additional selections need to be appropriate for the particular component of the FBA and have some basis in research to warrant inclusion. It will be noted that some of the strategies require little effort, time, or cost, such as *planned ignoring* where the teacher decides to ignore occurrences of noncompliance initially, and only respond to occurrences of cooperative behavior. Other interventions take considerable effort, time, or cost, such as a *curriculum change*, which may be necessary because too many of the students are failing in a particular subject, giving rise to problem behavior. A curriculum change intervention requires additional training and cost for materials. Obviously, in developing a plan, the teacher, specialist, or team members need to determine which strategies might not only be effective but *efficient*. It is up to the teachers to select the most appropriate strategies for their situation.

The strategies identified and described in this section have been listed in the following table, which comprises the content for Chapters 4, 5, 6, 7, and 8. The table represents a bank of strategies available for use in an intervention plan. The table is also included in the Appendices section (Appendix F: Bank of Strategies for Each FBA Component). The strategies for each component are listed alphabetically for ease of access and retrieval. In addition, the strategies include examples, citations, and additional resources.

In Chapter 7, Putting It All Together, guidelines are presented for selecting strategies for each component of the FBA components. Illustrations are also provided depicting the selection of strategies for the range of noncompliant behavior that a teacher is likely to encounter in a classroom. Finally, the three case studies introduced in Chapter 3 illustrating applications of an FBA will be completed with specific intervention plans. Chapter 8, the final chapter, presents a road map for educators summarizing the links between the FBA components and the bank for corresponding strategies. A glossary of terms for each strategy is also included to assist the reader in recalling the strategies.

Once the problem behavior, in this case noncompliance, has been identified and described in sufficient detail from the FBA information, the first level of intervention comes from the FBA component Immediate Triggers. The rationale for this starting point is that the triggers are immediately present to the teacher and can be directly addressed. If these strategies are effective, then the teacher will not need to use other, more time-consuming strategies related to Setting Events and Effects of Problem Behavior. A key assumption regarding *efficiency of intervention* is to begin with strategies addressing antecedents to the problem behavior—Immediate Triggers (Chapter 4), and Setting Events (Chapter 5), followed by strategies for addressing the Effects of Noncompliant Behavior (Chapter 6). In Chapter 7, guidelines are presented, with examples for developing systematic and comprehensive intervention plans.

Finally, the strategies for addressing the component Effects of Noncompliant Behavior, Chapter 6, are divided into two parts. The first part is directed toward strategies designed to establish the replacement behavior for noncompliance, specifically *cooperation*. The second part addresses specific strategies that have proven effectiveness in reducing or eliminating the problem behavior, *noncompliance*. In using these strategies, the reader is encouraged to develop a plan that shows a careful balance between strategies to increase expected behavior and reduce the target behavior.

Bank of Strategies for Each FBA Component (See Appendix F: Bank of Strategies for Each FBA Component)

Functional Behavioral Assessment Summary

Setting Events	Immediate Triggers		Problem Behavior		Effects of Problem Behavior

Intervention Plan

Setting Events	Immediate Triggers	Increasing Expected Behavior	Decreasing Problem Behavior

• Academic assessment and instructional decision making
• Anger management
• Conflict resolution
• Curriculum intervention
• Instructional delivery
• Individual behavior instruction plan
• Parent involvement
• Teacher-student relationship
• Self-management skills
• Social skills instruction
• Wraparound process
• Other
	Tier 1 Strategies
	  • Active supervision
	  • Behavioral momentum
	  • Defusing techniques
	  • Pacing
	  • Prompting
	  • Opportunities to respond
	  • Other
	
	Tier 2 Strategies
	  • Behavior rehearsal
	  • Context modification
	  • Fading
	  • Minimizing errors
	  • Precorrection
	  • Task interspersal
	  • Stimulus control
	  • Other
		• Focus on academic success
		• Behavioral contracts
		• Reinforcement
		  ○ Positive
		  ○ Negative
		  ○ Differential reinforcement
		• Shaping
		• Token economies
		• Other
			Tier 1 Strategies
			  • Maintain the flow of instruction
			  • Delayed responding
			  • Extinction
			  • Redirection prompts
			  • Rule restatement
			  • Other
			
			Tier 2 Strategies
			  • Part A: Establishing limits of behavior
			  • Part B: Conducting a debriefing session
			  • Other

4

Immediate Triggers

The strategies for this component of the functional behavioral assessment (FBA) and intervention plan, listed in Table 4.1, Strategies for Immediate Triggers, are designed to offset the triggering effects for whatever it is in the immediate environment that is setting off the noncompliant behavior. Because the triggers, by definition, precede the behavior, these strategies need to be applied *before* the triggers have a chance to function. In this sense, all of these strategies are *proactive* because they are implemented before the student(s) has a chance to exhibit problem behavior. The teacher or specialist, through information gathered in the FBA, is able to anticipate noncompliant behavior and intervene before problem behavior can occur. Clearly, the effectiveness of these strategies is very much dependent on *the timing of implementation*. The strategies must be implemented just prior to the presence of the triggers that may set off noncompliant behavior.

Some of the strategies take little time, effort, or cost and can readily be incorporated into the context of instruction. Other strategies will take more time and preparation, and, in some cases, cost. For this reason, the strategies are divided in two tiers. Tier 1 strategies require less time, effort, or cost, while Tier 2 strategies require more time, effort, or cost. Tier 1 strategies are used for early occurrences of noncompliant behavior, whereas Tier 2 strategies would be applied to situations when the behavior is more chronic and has been resistant to Tier 1 strategies. A brief illustration is provided with each strategy. The strategies are listed in alphabetical order.

Table 4.1 Strategies for Immediate Triggers (See Appendix F, Bank of Strategies for Each FBA Component)

Functional Behavioral Assessment Summary

Setting Events	Immediate Triggers	Problem Behavior	Effects of Problem Behavior

Intervention Plan

Setting Events	Immediate Triggers	Increasing Expected Behavior	Decreasing Problem Behavior
	Tier 1 Strategies • Active supervision • Behavioral momentum • Defusing techniques • Pacing • Prompting • Opportunities to respond • Other Tier 2 Strategies • Behavior rehearsal • Context modification • Fading • Minimizing errors • Precorrection • Task interspersal • Stimulus control • Other		

■ TIER 1 STRATEGIES: IMMEDIATE TRIGGERS

Active Supervision

Active supervision is a type of monitoring procedure used by teachers to maintain students' on-task behavior. The procedures typically involve (1) movement around the classroom to enable close proximity to all students at some point and to provide more frequent proximity to the student(s) who may exhibit noncompliance or other problem behavior, (2) scanning so that all students are observed on a regular basis, and (3) reasonably high rates of interaction with the students, especially the students likely to exhibit noncompliant behavior (Colvin, Sugai, Good, & Lee, 1997; Newcomer & Lewis, 2005).

Active supervision provides the teacher with an opportunity to deliver, in a timely manner, most of the following strategies described in this section and in subsequent chapters. This strategy should be a standard classroom practice for all teachers K–12.

BOX 4.1   ILLUSTRATION FOR ACTIVE SUPERVISION

The teacher Ms. Hailey directed the class to finish writing a paragraph by themselves. She then moved slowly down the aisles looking from side to side quietly acknowledging the students for starting quickly. She stood beside Enrico for a moment, as he usually does not do well with independent work, and praised him for getting started. Ms. Hailey then stopped, turned around, and watched the front half of the class. She continued to loop around the class, checking the students' work and making compliments here and there.

Behavioral Momentum

This strategy, behavioral momentum, is a metaphor taken from one of Newton's laws of motion, which describes the phenomenon of an object that, once set in motion, tends to stay in motion. In the classroom, once a student is cooperating and productively engaged with one task, there is more chance of the student cooperating and engaging in the task that immediately follows (Kern & Starosta, 2004). This strategy also has had wide application for students with disabilities who have difficulty following directions (Belfiore, Pulley Basile, & Lee, 2008). In addition, the strategy is particularly useful when a student exhibits avoidance behavior with a particular task.

BOX 4.2   ILLUSTRATION FOR BEHAVIORAL MOMENTUM

Michael does not like to read, so when he has to read he puts his head on his desk and closes his eyes. His teacher, on this occasion, reads to him for a couple of minutes and engages his attention. She then asks him to read with her, which he does, and he is then asked to read a little by himself. He continues to read and the teacher praises him.

Defusing Techniques

Sometimes students become agitated or upset over something and cannot settle down, which makes instruction difficult for them, and it is possible that the student may escalate to more serious behavior. Colvin (2004) fully described an array of defusing strategies designed to reduce student agitation (such as showing teacher empathy, presenting options, assisting the student to focus on the present task, providing space, providing assurances and additional time as appropriate, using preferred activities, providing accommodations, using teacher proximity, providing independent activities, engaging in low-demand activities, using movement tasks, and including self-management activities). These strategies are important for teachers to use because when students are agitated, they are highly likely to engage in noncompliant and other problem behavior.

BOX 4.3   ILLUSTRATION FOR DEFUSING TECHNIQUES

Sarah had that serious look on her face and was starting to complain about the school, the class, and students (this is her pattern, and usually it is not long before she is arguing and refusing to do any work). The teacher, on seeing the initial signs of agitation, approached her and asked her if she needed help or needed some quiet time to herself. She said quiet time. The teacher suggested she put her head down for a few minutes and that she would check on her shortly.

Pacing

Good pacing is an instructional technique used by teachers to maintain the flow of instruction. Specifically, it is a measure of the *rate* of instructional delivery tied to three areas: (1) the time taken for teachers to present information; (2) the time taken for students to complete a task; and (3) the time between students' completion of a task and the teacher's presentation of further information or tasks (Engelmann & Carnine, 1991). There is a solid body of research that links good pacing with high rates of student on-task behavior, and conversely, slow pacing with off-task and disruptive behavior (Darch & Kame'enui, 2004).

BOX 4.4   ILLUSTRATION FOR PACING

The math teacher was presenting information on how to solve a problem. She secured the class's attention and delivered the information in a brisk manner (not rushed but quickly enough so that the students were able to follow). She told the class that they have five minutes to complete the first two problems. After five minutes were up, the teacher secured their attention again, checked whether they were on track with the problem-solving strategy, and then directed them to complete the remaining four problems in their text.

Note: The teacher provided the initial information at a reasonably fast pace, gave the students sufficient time to complete the task but not too much time, and there was no down time from when the students finished the task to when the teacher checked their work.

Prompting

This technique involves providing additional information, such as a hint, cue, or gesture, to a student just prior to engaging the student in a task. The prompt assists the student to make the correct response and also helps to interrupt a student who may be about to make an incorrect response (Colvin, 2004). This strategy is an effective tool for helping students who display chronic problem behavior. The reason is that in a given context where the problem behavior is likely to occur, the prompt helps the student to focus on the expected behavior (VanDerHeyden, 2005). The key for effective use of prompting is *timing*. The prompt must be delivered either prior to the student having an opportunity to make an error or exhibit problem behavior, or at the early onset of the occurrence of an error or problem behavior.

A variation of prompting is known as *advance prompting*. In this case, the teacher provides the prompt well ahead of time so that students become aware that change will soon occur. Advance prompts are very useful for helping students make difficult transitions. Prompting is also an example of a generic intervention, Weakening Stimulus Control, described in the Tier 2 strategies of this section.

BOX 4.5   ILLUSTRATION FOR PROMPTING

Michael has a hard time with silent reading. He is usually engaged quite productively in class, but often when the teacher announces it is time to switch to silent reading, he starts to fidget, whine, and become argumentative. The teacher stands near him and announces to the class, "In a couple of minutes we will be switching over to reading, so please see if you can finish what you are doing" (advance prompt). Shortly after, the teacher directs the class to take out their reading books. She approaches Michael, who is starting to fidget, and puts her fingers to her lips and whispers, "Michael, let's get started on the reading. You can do it." He grimaces and pulls out a book. The teacher responds, "Atta boy. Thanks."

Opportunities to Respond

If students are productively engaged in their work, there is less chance of problem behavior (Sutherland, 2003). Clearly, if students are required to sit for lengthy periods of time, especially students with problem behavior, without the opportunity to respond or participate, there will be problems. Similarly, Frase and Hetzel (1990) reported, "The first seven minutes are predictive of how the rest of the lesson will proceed" (pp. 77–78). In addition, especially early in the lesson, students need to have the opportunity to respond *correctly*. Typically, teachers who keep instruction moving also pair this technique of providing Opportunities to Respond with the strategy of maintaining good Pacing described earlier in this section. This combination helps to ensure high rates of on-task behavior.

BOX 4.6   ILLUSTRATION FOR OPPORTUNITIES TO RESPOND

Shortly after science class started, the teacher announced, "We have a small block of ice and the same sized block of butter. Tell your neighbor which one would melt first." A few seconds later, the teacher said, "Please write down, in one sentence, an explanation for your answer." A few minutes later, the teacher told the students to share with their neighbor what they have written. Shortly thereafter, the teacher called on one student to tell the class her answer. The teacher then asked the class to raise their hand if they agreed with this answer. Then the teacher asked if anyone disagreed, and so on.

Note: Each of these activities in the lesson required responses from all students.

Other

As noted earlier, it is important to understand that the strategies included are not meant to be exhaustive. Rather, they are intended to represent a reasonable compilation of established evidence-based practices. Teachers and specialists are strongly encouraged to add strategies to these lists that they have found to be useful with the proviso that these additional selections are appropriate for the particular component of the functional behavioral assessment and have some basis in research to warrant inclusion.

TIER 2 STRATEGIES: IMMEDIATE TRIGGERS ■

As noted earlier, these strategies typically take more time, effort, or cost. The usual practice is to use Tier 1 strategies first, and then if these strategies are not successful in changing behavior, implement the Tier 2 strategies. If the noncompliant behavior was particularly severe and intense, the teacher might go straight to Tier 2 strategies.

Behavioral Rehearsal

In this strategy, the teacher creates approximations of the settings or context that is likely to trigger noncompliance (Cartledge, 2005). Behavioral rehearsal has wide application for students who have fears or other avoidance responses to certain situations or who are not fluent with responding, and for students who display strong emotional reactive behavior in specific contexts. An important advantage in using this strategy is that it puts the teacher in a supportive versus adversarial role. In addition, the contrived context is often less threatening to the student than the actual context. Behavioral rehearsal typically involves three steps: (1) creating the context or stimuli that is likely to trigger the problem behavior; (2) assisting the student to complete the directed task in this context; and (3) transitioning from the contrived context to the real situation.

BOX 4.7   ILLUSTRATION FOR BEHAVIORAL REHEARSAL

Dennis always balks when oral reading occurs. Usually when it is his turn he refuses to read and has at times created such a scene that he has had to be removed from the reading group. The teacher took him aside one day and told him that they were going to do some reading together and it would be just the two of them. The teacher picked a quiet spot in the room and told him that she would read first, then they would read together, and then he would read a little by himself. They performed this routine a few times until he was quite fluent and showed no signs of resisting. The teacher then brought over another student, telling Dennis that this person needs to practice some reading with them. The same routine was repeated. This behavioral rehearsal was conducted several times during the week until Dennis was quite fluent and comfortable reading with another student present. During this time, he was not required to read orally in the class group. After the next session, Dennis was told that he is doing really well and that he could easily take a turn in the reading group, which was coming up shortly. In the reading group, Dennis was called on to read a sentence following the same person he had been reading with during the behavioral rehearsal group. The amount of reading in the group for Dennis was then systematically increased until it matched the length of time the other students were reading.

Context Modification

Context modification is a relatively simple strategy designed to slightly change the setting where the noncompliant behavior occurs so that the student is more likely to exhibit the expected behavior and less likely to be noncompliant (Colvin, 2004). Context modification can involve a number of changes, such as reducing the amount of work or number of examples that a student needs to complete; spending less time on the more difficult or challenging tasks; altering the physical conditions such as seating arrangements; and rearranging the schedule so that the more difficult tasks are presented at a different time of day. Two steps are typically undertaken in using context modification as a strategy in the classroom: (1) alter the context that is likely to trigger the problem behavior and maintain this context until the student successfully completes the expected behavior and (2) systematically change the context back to the original or normal context where the problems arose initially.

BOX 4.8   ILLUSTRATION FOR CONTEXT MODIFICATION

Roseanne becomes argumentative and noncompliant during independent work in math. The teacher visits with her and discusses the issues she has when it is time to work by herself. She quickly says, "I cannot do math, that's why." Her teacher points out that all she is asked to do is to get started and then she can get some help (the teacher has reliable information from previous work that she can do the math). Roseanne is asked to get out her math notebook and put a date on the page. She is then asked to make an attempt at the first problem, which she does and the teacher acknowledges her cooperation. The teacher then asks her to complete the next two problems herself and raise her hand when she is done. Meanwhile, the rest of the class is working independently on the ten exercises in the math book. Roseanne completes the two questions as directed. The teacher then tells her that all she needs to do this day is to complete three more questions and turn them in. The teacher continues this procedure, gradually increasing the amount of work that Roseanne is expected to do as she is more successful in working independently and reducing the amount of attention she is giving her.

Fading

Fading is a very important strategy to use in managing noncompliance because interventions used to address noncompliance usually involve some change in the original setting, either the task itself or in the environment. It was noted in Chapter 2 that noncompliant behavior is usually reinforced and maintained by changes in or removal of the demand situation. Consequently, an intervention introduced by the teacher usually results in a change of the demand situation, even though the goal is to have the student cooperate and complete the task successfully. In this sense, the intervention may reinforce noncompliant behavior as well because the original demand has been altered. Thus, when the teacher tries to resume the normal demand situation, noncompliance may be exhibited again. The emergence of noncompliance is even more likely if the teacher simply drops the intervention and returns to the normal cues and levels of assistance used in the classroom (Albin, 2005; Engelmann & Carnine, 1991). The basic approach in fading an intervention is to use four steps: (1) carefully examine the levels of assistance provided in the intervention after the student demonstrates success; (2) examine the level of support provided in the normal classroom setting for all students; (3) identify some intermediate levels of support between what is provided during the intervention (most) to what is available in the normal classroom setting (least); and (4) systematically provide support from most support (intervention level) to intermediate levels (fading) to the least support levels (normal classroom support).

BOX 4.9 ILLUSTRATION FOR FADING

Carlos exhibits off-task behavior during independent work and becomes noncompliant when he is directed to resume his work. The teacher decides to give him more assistance and attention at the beginning of independent work to help him get started. The teacher stands near him, prompts him to get started, acknowledges the quick start, and watches him work for a while (intervention). Once Carlos successfully commences the independent work and completes a few examples, the teacher begins to fade his level of assistance by providing less assistance at the start, standing near him for less time, and providing less acknowledgment for working. When Carlos is successful with this reduced level of assistance, the teacher fades his contact and presence even more by standing near Carlos just briefly, watches his start, goes to other students, and comes back to him. The teacher then moves to the final component (again based on the student being successful with the previous level of support) to the practice used for the class, which is to explain the task to be completed independently and then to move around the room with intermittent contact and praise for students on-task, providing assistance as needed.

Minimizing Errors

Some students have a strong aversion for making errors during instruction. So, when new learning is introduced, there is a high chance of errors occurring. Consequently, some students will display noncompliance and other avoidance behavior rather than commit errors. Some steps taken to minimize errors during instruction include ensuring that the directions presented are very clear; designing skill sequences carefully to ensure the students have mastered the prerequisite skills; using sufficient examples for practice to guarantee mastery of the skills being taught; delivering instruction to ensure students know what is required of them with adequate modeling from the teacher, opportunities to respond, and timely correction procedures (Engelmann & Colvin, 2007; Wolery, 2005). In addition, a common practice for teachers who have students who avoid making errors is to separate work completion from work correction. In these cases, the teacher acknowledges the students for completing their work and tells them it will be corrected next period or later in the day.

BOX 4.10   ILLUSTRATION FOR MINIMIZING ERRORS

Sonia was one of those students who would only work on content she was really certain she could do without mistakes. With new work or even work she might be able to complete, she would shut down and refuse to cooperate. The teacher checked out her skill levels in various reading comprehension tasks and found that she was quite firm in some areas and weak in others. The teacher then designed a step-by-step reading program with her that walked her through the prerequisite skills, providing high levels of modeling and practice for her. In a relatively short time, Sonia was participating actively in the reading comprehension class at the level of other students.

Precorrection

Precorrection is one of the simplest and most effective proactive strategies to use for addressing problem behavior. The strategy is based on knowing the triggers that set off the problem behavior and intervening before the student is exposed to these triggers (Colvin, 2005b). A range of precorrection measures are available. Tier 1 applications can be as simple as providing a reminder just before the student is presented with the triggers, whereas Tier 2 formal plans involve a number of steps. For example, Colvin (2004) developed a seven-step precorrection plan: (1) identify the triggers and the predictable problem behavior; (2) clearly specify the expected or cooperative behavior; (3) modify the context to minimize the effects of the triggers; (4) provide practice opportunities for the cooperative behavior prior to entering the target setting; (5) prompt expected behavior in the target setting as needed; (6) deliver strong reinforcement for displays of the expected cooperative behavior in the target setting; and (7) monitor and evaluate the plan.

BOX 4.11   ILLUSTRATION FOR PRECORRECTION

Melanie liked to use the computer. However, when it was time to end her session on the computer and go to her desk, she would refuse. The teacher identified that Melanie's transition from the preferred activity to her desk was the trigger, and her refusal to follow the direction was the problem behavior. The teacher visited with her and explained that using the computer is a privilege and that she needs to quit when her time is up, otherwise she may lose the privilege. The next time Melanie went to use the computer, the teacher reminded her of the need to quit on time. A few minutes before Melanie's time was up on the computer, the teacher went to her and interacted a little, then mentioned that in a few minutes her time would be up and to see if she could make the effort to cooperate. When her time was up, Melanie went to her desk, and the teacher praised her for her cooperation.

Task Interspersal

Some students may get started with an academic task or activity and then quit and become noncompliant when they run into difficulty. Task interspersal is a strategy designed to include easier and more reinforcing tasks with a series of harder tasks (Kern & Clemens, 2005). By interspersing easier tasks with the more difficult tasks, the student is more likely to be successful and to keep on task. For example, if the target or difficult task is A, and the easier tasks are B, C, and D, then an interspersal sequence could be: AABCACDAACDAB. . . . In this way, the student experiences task completion as well as a much higher success rate overall compared with working on the hard examples alone. It is desirable to use previously mastered tasks as the easier tasks, which provide the student with the opportunity to practice and maintain mastery of these skills. However, the amount of interspersal skills should be faded once the student is able to work more successfully with difficult tasks. The reason is that a review of research by Cates (2005) showed that the task interspersal strategy may slow down learning. Teachers have often combined task interspersal with the behavioral momentum strategies described earlier in this section.

BOX 4.12 ILLUSTRATION FOR TASK DISPERSAL

Emily was an average student at math, but when she had to work on more difficult problems, she would work for a while and then quit and become quite resistant to directions and offers for assistance from the teacher. On this occasion, she was to begin work on three-digit multiplication problems. She had already mastered multiplication with two-digit and one-digit examples. The teacher arranged her work so that the examples included a mix of three-digit, two-digit, and one-digit problems. The sequence included more two-digit and one-digit problems than three-digit examples. Emily was asked to raise her hand when she had finished the series of problems. The teacher made a point of praising her strongly for finishing the problems. This series was repeated, and the teacher increased the ratio of the hard problems to the easier ones, ensuring that Emily was successful in completing the work each time. Eventually, Emily was able to complete a full series of the three-digit problems successfully.

Stimulus Control

Stimulus control is a useful concept coming from the early operant behavioral literature for describing the predictable relationship between a given stimulus and a response (Luiselli, 2005). By weakening the stimulus control between the stimulus (trigger) and the response (problem behavior), the student will have more chance to exhibit other behaviors versus the problem behavior. Typically, there are four steps in using the stimulus control paradigm to address a problem behavior: (1) identify the specific stimulus that sets the occasion for the problem behavior; (2) carefully examine and identify the features of the stimulus, especially those features that can be manipulated; (3) systematically alter the features of the stimulus so as to weaken the stimulus control; and (4) fade changes to resume initial stimulus features as appropriate.

> **BOX 4.13   ILLUSTRATION FOR WEAKENING STIMULUS CONTROL**
>
> It was quite evident that when Juan was required to correct his work, he would become belligerent and noncompliant. The teacher carefully examined the language she was using with Juan when work was being corrected, how much work he was required to correct, and the details of the responses required of Juan to correct his work. The teacher made several changes prior to the next occasion when Juan would have to correct his work. The teacher told Juan that they were going to do things differently this time in that the teacher would correct the first problem and Juan would be required to watch. The teacher then gave the pencil to Juan, asking him to make the changes she suggested. For the third and last correction, the teacher wrote down the corrections and asked Juan to copy the changes. The teacher noted that she was able to get through the corrections this way without any belligerence or resistance. These steps were followed a few more times. The teacher then faded out some of the steps used to assist Juan and encouraged him to correct more of his work by himself. The teacher found that once he was able to "get over the hump" of correcting his work by changing the manner in which the work was corrected, it was not long before he was able to follow the correction procedures used by the rest of the class.

Other

Teachers and specialists are strongly encouraged to add strategies to the lists that they have found to be useful with the proviso that these additional selections are appropriate for the particular component of the FBA and have some basis in research to warrant inclusion.

■ CHAPTER SUMMARY

Immediate Triggers is the first component to be addressed in designing interventions for noncompliant behavior. These measures are *proactive* by definition because they are implemented *before* the student has a chance to respond. All of the strategies are evidence-based and have been documented with additional references. The strategies have been divided into two tiers based on ease of implementation with respect to time, effort, or cost.

5

Setting Events

Setting Events are those factors that may contribute to the problem behavior in terms of a spillover or buildup effect. They set the occasion for the problem behavior. For example, a student may be having problems at home, which may carry over to problem behavior at school; another student may have medical issues that will influence behavior at school; a third student may have failed the last two quizzes and may refuse to cooperate in getting ready for the next one. It is very important to realize that the relationship between Setting Events and problem behavior is *speculative.* This means that strategies used to address the identified Setting Events may or may not change the problem behavior in the target setting. The student's behavioral performance and data will provide information on whether this strategy is effective or not. However, the strategies typically used to attend to Setting Events are designed to meet an evident need of the student. In this sense the student will still benefit from the support.

Strategies used to intervene with Setting Events, listed in Table 5.1, Strategies for Setting Events (see Appendix F: Bank of Strategies for Each FBA Component), usually take considerable time, effort, and, in some cases, cost. For these reasons, the strategies are typically used when the less intrusive measures designed to address the Immediate Triggers and Effects of Problem Behavior have not changed the problem behavior. It is also important to gather reliable information on the student's needs in order to select the most appropriate strategy. Because these strategies generally involve formal program type interventions and a high level of coordination, additional resources are recommended.

Academic Assessment and Instructional Decision Making

The most common context for students to exhibit noncompliance in the classroom is during instruction and teacher-led activities. This is to be

Table 5.1 Strategies for Setting Events (See Appendix F: Bank of Strategies for Each FBA Component)

Functional Behavioral Assessment Summary			
Setting Events	*Immediate Triggers*	*Problem Behavior*	*Effects of Problem Behavior*

Intervention Plan			
Setting Events	*Immediate Triggers*	*Increasing Expected Behavior*	*Decreasing Problem Behavior*
• Academic assessment and instructional decision making • Anger management • Conflict resolution • Curriculum intervention • Instructional delivery • Individual behavior instruction plan • Parent involvement • Teacher-student relationship • Self-management skills • Social skills instruction • Wraparound process • Other			

expected because students spend most of their classroom time in instruction (if not we would have a very different problem!). When students exhibit noncompliance on any regular basis during instruction, a reasonable conclusion is that these students are endeavoring to *avoid the instructional task.* Consequently, a crucial question for the teacher in trying to address noncompliant behavior is to ask, "Can the student perform the task," or, "Does the student have the skills necessary to complete the task satisfactorily?" Clearly, it would be pointless to undertake positive interventions such as incentives, contracts, and precorrection, or provide negative consequences for lack of cooperation, if the student cannot perform the task. An appropriate intervention would be to help the student perform the task by providing additional instructional support.

When students noncomply during instruction, the teacher needs to make the following determination: if the student can perform the task but will not, then we have noncompliance. However, if the student cannot perform the task and will not, then we have an instructional problem. There are two steps usually taken to help teachers make this determination: (1) assess whether the student has the necessary skills to perform the task satisfactorily, and, (2) based on this assessment, make instructional adjustments so that the student receives support to perform the skills, or adjust the task to match the student's skill level. To accomplish these steps, teachers need to become fluent with ongoing academic assessment and to make instructional decisions based on these assessment results. Another approach teachers can take when the student does not cooperate with a task is to present a task that the teacher is quite certain the student can perform. If the student cooperates with this task and not the previous one, then the teacher can conclude the student cannot perform the task. However, if the student refuses to cooperate with the known task, then the teacher may conclude the student is being noncompliant.

Resources designed to describe these assessment issues are provided in Box 5.1.

BOX 5.1   RESOURCES FOR ACADEMIC ASSESSMENT AND INSTRUCTIONAL DECISION MAKING

Shapiro, E. S. (2004). *Academic skills: Direct assessment and intervention.* New York: Guilford Press.

Stiggins, R. J. (2001). *Student-involved student assessment* (3rd ed.). Columbus, OH: Merrill Prentice Hall.

Tindal, G., & Haladyna, T. M. (Eds.). (2002). *Large scale assessment programs for all students: Validity, technical adequacy and implementation.* Mahwah, NJ: Lawrence Erlbaum Associates.

Anger Management

One of the characteristic features of students who show antisocial behavior in school is that they carry high levels of anger. Many have great difficulty controlling and managing their anger effectively, which can often lead to a range of problem behavior from noncompliance and disruption to serious conflicts and outbursts. It becomes very difficult, if not futile in some cases, to address noncompliance in the classroom when it is enmeshed with a host of other serious behaviors in this overall pattern of angry and aggressive behavior. These students need systematic and comprehensive training in anger management so that they can learn how to recognize and control their anger and to avoid initiating and escalating conflicts and severe problem behavior.

Studies identified in the resources listed below have demonstrated that anger management techniques can be taught effectively to the full range of school populations, K–12. These techniques can be delivered in classrooms to the whole class, to small groups of students, or to individual students, depending on the need. Several resources for teaching anger management are listed in Box 5.2 for teachers and specialists to adopt or adapt in their classrooms as appropriate.

BOX 5.2   RESOURCES FOR TEACHING ANGER MANAGEMENT STRATEGIES IN THE CLASSROOM

Carr, T. (2005). *141 creative strategies for reaching adolescents with anger problems.* Chapin, NC: Youthlight, Inc.

Colvin, G. (1999). *Defusing anger and aggression: Safe strategies for secondary school educators* [Video/DVD program]. Eugene, OR: Iris Media.

Marion, M. (1997). Guiding young children's understanding and management of anger. *Young Children, 52* (7), 62–67.

Stewart, J. (2002). *The anger workbook for teens.* Torrance, CA: Jalmar Press.

Conflict Resolution

Another common feature of students who exhibit antisocial behavior is the inability to get along with their peers and to cooperate with adults. Conflicts often arise because younger students do not have the skills to share, play together, or solve problems. Similarly, older students will not negotiate with their peers and become quite antiauthoritarian with adults. At the core of these problems is the need to develop skills in the areas of conflict resolution and problem solving. If these students were able to solve problems and conflicts peacefully, and they could learn to get along with their peers and cooperate with adults, they could be successful in school. If not, the prognosis leans toward failure in school and ultimately dropping out of school. Schoolwide practices have been adopted to help students solve conflicts such as peer mediation, student conflict resolvers, and peaceable school plans. Several published programs, curriculum materials, and texts are available to help teachers provide instruction and develop systems for conflict resolution. Some of these resources are listed in Box 5.3.

BOX 5.3   RESOURCES FOR TEACHING CONFLICT RESOLUTION SKILLS

Cohen, R. (1995). *Students resolving conflict: Peer mediation in schools.* Tucson, AZ: Good Year Books.

Girard, K., & Koch, S. J. (1996). *Conflict resolution in the schools: A manual for educators.* San Francisco: Jossey-Bass Publishers.

Walker, H., Colvin, G., & Ramsey, E. (1995). *Antisocial behavior in school: Strategies and best practices.* Pacific Grove, CA: Brooks/Cole.

Curriculum Intervention

It was noted in Chapter 3 that a major motivation for students who display noncompliance in the classroom is to *avoid* or *escape from* their work. In some cases they avoid their work simply because they have not learned sufficient skills to be able to successfully participate in the lesson. One significant reason for students not having learned the necessary skills is that the curricula used by the teachers may be poorly designed. This means teachers may be working very diligently to have the students learn but that students fail to learn as a result of an inadequate curriculum. Engelmann (1993) clearly articulated a number of reasons why a curriculum may be flawed and cause students to fail, such as uneven sequencing of component skills; insufficient practice examples to ensure mastery; ambiguous communication of rules; directions for completing exercises are unclear; skills learned in one lesson do not apply to the next lesson and may even contradict skills presented in later lessons; examples do not sample the universe so students cannot generalize to other examples; insufficient application of examples and rules for students to fully understand the concept or operation; and insufficient review of previously learned skills so the skills are forgotten. Clearly, it is a formidable task to design an effective and efficient curriculum. However, if several students in a class are having problems, the teacher should evaluate the curriculum and replace it if necessary. In some cases, it may be possible to make adaptations to the curriculum used or to add components from other curricula. The resources in Box 5.4 provide additional information for addressing the appropriateness of a curriculum and guidelines for making changes as necessary.

BOX 5.4   RESOURCES FOR CURRICULUM INTERVENTIONS

Engelmann, S. (1993). The curriculum as the cause of failure. In J. Marr, G. Sugai, & G. Tindal (Eds.), *The Oregon conference monograph 1993* (pp. 3–8). Eugene, OR: University of Oregon, College of Education.

Print, M. (1993). *Curriculum development and design.* Sydney, Australia: Allen & Unwin Book Publishers.

Sprague, J. R., & Golly, A. (2004). *Best behavior: Building positive behavior support in schools.* Longmont, CO: Sopris West Educational Services.

Instructional Delivery

Although there are many reasons for students exhibiting noncompliance and avoiding their work in school, one factor is paramount for addressing this issue, and that is effective instructional delivery. If the teacher's instruction is delivered in an engaging and focused manner, there is more likelihood that students will be productively engaged, and cooperative behavior will prevail in the classroom. However, a given teacher's style of instruction may be effective for most students but not for a student with problem behavior. In these cases, the teacher will need to make some adjustments in order to engage these students. There are many adjustments that can be made to the way in which instruction is delivered. Some of these have already been addressed, including pacing, opportunities to respond, and a focused first few minutes of the lesson. Additional strategies include planned variations of instruction, ranging from the whole class to small group to independent work; balancing reading, writing, discussion, and explanations; effective correction procedures; establishing classroom routines; cooperative learning procedures; and questioning and answering routines. If one or more students are not responding to the teacher's delivery of instruction, then adjustments need to occur and careful attention needs to be paid to these students to gauge their levels of response. Box 5.5 lists a few sources for information on techniques for delivering and adapting instruction.

BOX 5.5   RESOURCES FOR INSTRUCTIONAL DELIVERY

Colvin, G., & Lazar, M. (1997). *The effective elementary classroom: Managing for success.* Longmont, CO: Sopris West.

Cotton, K. (2000). *The schooling practices that matter most.* Alexandria, VA: Association for Supervision and Curriculum Development.

Hunter, R. (2004). *Madeline Hunter's mastery teaching.* Thousand Oaks, CA: Corwin.

Individual Behavior Instruction Plan

This strategy rests on a simple assumption that students who exhibit chronic noncompliance have not learned the expected behavior of following directions (or that they have learned the wrong way). Behavior instruction plans are designed on the basis that following an expected behavior is a skill to be learned, and for that matter, a skill to be taught. This approach is very effective, but it does take time to prepare the plan, visit with the student, and monitor its implementation. However, the results for the students are usually well worth the additional effort required by the teacher in using this strategy. The primary focus of the behavior instruction plan is to teach a replacement behavior for noncompliance, which is cooperative behavior. The steps in developing a behavior instruction plan for younger and older students are elaborated in the resources cited in Box 5.6.

BOX 5.6   RESOURCES FOR INDIVIDUAL BEHAVIOR INSTRUCTION PLANS

Colvin, G. (2004). *Managing the cycle of acting-out behavior in the classroom.* Eugene, OR: Behavior Associates.

Hieneman, M., Nolan, M., Presley, J., De Turo, L., Roberson, W., & Dunlap, G. (1999). *Facilitator's guide: Positive behavioral support.* Tallahassee, FL: Positive Behavioral Support Project, Florida Department of Education.

Sprick, R., & Garrison, M. (2008). *Interventions: Evidence-based behavioral strategies for individual students* (2nd ed.). Eugene, OR: Pacific Northwest Publishing.

Sprick, R., Garrison, M., & Howard, L. (1998). *CHAMPs: A proactive and positive approach to classroom management.* Longmont, CO: Sopris West.

Parent Involvement

Educators and researchers have reported over many years on the central role that family and home play in the formation of both desirable and undesirable behavior with children. Consequently, it is imperative to take whatever measures possible to enlist *parent involvement* in the support of school or classroom interventions for students with noncompliant behavior. Typically, students who display noncompliance at school also show the same behaviors, perhaps in different ways, at home. Therefore, it is to everyone's benefit for parents and school staff to work closely together, in a partnership, to develop and implement an intervention plan that cuts across both school and home. Ideally, parents participate in the planning and implementation of the intervention plan. Also, a reliable communication system must be established so that the parents and teachers can communicate in an ongoing and timely manner. Several effective parent-school partnership programs have been developed over the years for addressing students with problem behavior in school and home, some of which are listed in Box 5.7.

BOX 5.7   RESOURCES FOR PARENT INVOLVEMENT

Epstein, J. L., Sanders, M. G., Simon, B. S., Clark Salinas, N., Rodriguez Jansorn, N., & Van Voorhis, F. L. (2002). *School, family, and community partnerships: Your handbook for action.* Thousand Oaks, CA: Corwin.

Forgatch, M. S., & Patterson, G. R. (2005). *Parents and adolescents living together: Part 2. Family problem solving* (2nd ed.). Champaign, IL: Research Press.

Patterson, G. R., & Forgatch, M. S. (2005). *Parents and adolescents living together: Part 1: The basics* (2nd ed.). Champaign, IL: Research Press.

Walker, H., Colvin, G., & Ramsey, E. (1995). *Antisocial behavior in school: Strategies and best practice.* Pacific Grove, CA: Brooks/Cole.

Teacher-Student Relationship

Some students persist with noncompliant behavior in the classroom simply on the basis that they *don't like the teacher.* These students often show hostility toward their teacher and will thwart efforts by their teacher to improve cooperative behavior in the classroom. In general, the quality of the teacher-student relationship is an important motivational factor for students to improve and maintain desirable behavior and academic performance in the classroom, although there are limits to such relationships. The typical goal for teachers is to serve as good role models and communicate to their students that they are trustworthy, care for their personal and social well-being, and want them to succeed academically and socially in their classroom. Generally, if students perceive that their teacher has their best interests at heart, they will respond more to this teacher. Unfortunately, teachers often report that they want the best for their students and believe they demonstrate care and concern for them. However, we are dealing with *perceptions.* This means that the students' perceptions of the teachers' behavior toward them is negative. In order to deal with student negative perceptions of the teacher' regard for them, several steps can be taken, which are fully described in the selected resources in Box 5.8.

BOX 5.8   RESOURCES FOR TEACHER-STUDENT RELATIONSHIPS

Diffily, D., & Sassman, C. (2006). *Positive teacher talk for better classroom management, grades K–2.* New York: Scholastic.

Jones, V. F., & Jones, J. (2006). *Comprehensive classroom management: Creating communities of support and problem solving.* Boston: Allyn & Bacon.

Starkman, N. (2006). *Connecting in your classroom: 18 teachers tell how they foster the relationships that lead to student success.* Minneapolis, MN: Search Institute.

Self-Management Skills

Some of the students who exhibit high rates of noncompliant behavior in the classroom have been described as stubborn, strong-willed, and as having minds of their own. These students often take charge of a situation by acting inappropriately and, in some cases, leading others to act inappropriately. Their noncompliant behavior is reinforced by causing predictable responses or reactions from others that are generally inappropriate. If this desire to control their environment could be channeled toward productive and acceptable behavior, then these students could become successful in school and in life. One strategy for steering students in this direction is to establish *self-management skills* with the students. This is a well-documented strategy for helping students change problem behavior to acceptable behavior and also for improving academic performance.

A self-management program basically puts the student in charge of an intervention that is typically administered by the teacher. However, it is most important to understand that the teacher is not simply handing the responsibility over to the student. This will not work. Rather, the teacher needs to take systematic steps to teach the student all the steps involved in assessing the problem, targeting the noncompliant behavior, setting a goal for cooperative behavior, developing structures so students can remind themselves of what they are expected to do, developing alternative strategies to the triggers that set off the noncompliant behavior, establishing a monitoring and evaluation plan, and developing self-reinforcement plans for successes. Details for these steps, or variations of these steps, are described in the resources found in Box 5.9.

BOX 5.9   RESOURCES FOR SELF-MANAGEMENT SKILLS

Cummings, C. (2000). *Winning strategies for classroom management.* Alexandria, VA: Association for Supervision and Curriculum Development.

Shapiro, E. S. (1994). *Behavior change in the classroom: Self-management interventions.* New York: Guilford Press.

Young, K. R., West, R. P., Smith, D. J., & Morgan, D. P. (1991). *Teaching self-management strategies to adolescents.* Longmont, CO: Sopris West.

Social Skills Instruction

Students who display chronic noncompliant behavior are often described as antisocial. The reason is clear. If they are noncompliant or noncooperative with their peers, then it is not long before they become rejected or isolated from their peers, which brings on antisocial behavior. Similarly, if they are noncompliant and noncooperative with their teachers, then they will receive less social approval and positive interactions from their teachers, which can lead to further alienation in the classroom. Instructional activities such as sharing, cooperative learning, listening, taking a turn, getting along with others, and following directions all require social competence. One of the surest strategies for addressing antisocial behavior is to formally teach *social skills* to these students. The approach to teaching social skills and to helping students achieve social competence is fundamentally the same as for teaching academic skills. The assumption is that social skills are behaviors that can be *taught*. Many social skills curricula are available; no one curriculum can be expected to address the specific needs of all students in a given classroom. Teachers will need to take a curriculum that has appeal and adapt the content and activities to meet the needs of their particular students. Some social skills resources are listed in Box 5.10.

BOX 5.10   RESOURCES FOR SOCIAL SKILLS INSTRUCTION

Dowd, T., & Tierney, J. (2005). *Teaching social skills to youth* (2nd ed.). Boys Town, NE: Boys Town Press.
Knoff, H. M. (2001). *Stop and think social skills program.* Longmont, CO: Sopris West.
McGinnis, E., & Goldstein, A. P. (2003). *Skillstreaming in early childhood: New strategies for teaching prosocial social skills* (Rev. ed.). Champaign, IL: Research Press.

Wraparound Process

Some students display variations of persistent noncompliant behavior not only at school, but also at home and in the community. Students in trouble with law enforcement, in a very serious sense, are exhibiting noncompliant behavior. Essentially, wraparound, as the name suggests, is an integrated approach to providing assistance to students with pervasive noncompliant behavior and other problem behavior. The process encompasses building effective working relationships and support networks for students, their families, teachers, school support personnel, and any involved agencies and support services. Typically, a facilitator is needed to coordinate the process, roles of participants are carefully defined, monitoring and reporting procedures are established, all key environments and problem behaviors are targeted, and a comprehensive support plan is developed and implemented by all stakeholders. Detailed steps for developing and implementing a wraparound approach are listed in Box 5.11.

BOX 5.11   RESOURCES FOR WRAPAROUND PROCESS

Burns, B. J., & Goldman, S. K. (1999). *Promising practices in wraparound for children with serious emotional disturbance and their families: Systems of care.* Washington, DC: Center for Effective Collaboration and Practice, American Institute for Research.
Eber, L. (2003). *The art and science of wraparound: Completing the continuum of schoolwide behavioral support.* Bloomington, IN: Forum on Education at Indiana University.
Eber, L., Hyde, K., Rose, J., Breen, K., McDonald, D., & Lewandowski, H. (2008). Completing the continuum of school-wide positive behavior support: Wraparound as a tertiary level intervention. In W. Sailor, G. Dunlap, G. Sugai, & R. Horner (Eds.), *Handbook of positive behavior support.* New York: Springer.

Other

Teachers and specialists are strongly encouraged to add strategies to these lists that they have found to be useful with the proviso that these additional selections are appropriate for the particular component of the FBA and have some basis in research to warrant inclusion.

■ CHAPTER SUMMARY

It is well known among educators that issues outside of the classroom can have significant bearing on problem behavior exhibited by students at school and in the classroom. In addition, previous experiences with an activity or subject can impact student behavior. If standard strategies implemented in the classroom are not effective in changing the student's noncompliant behavior, then the teacher or specialist will need to address setting events. Moreover, if the FBA information identifies setting events that are highly likely to affect student behavior, these setting events will need to be targeted in the intervention plan.

It needs to be understood, in addressing setting events, that there is an element of *speculation* in proposing that the setting event is functionally related to the student noncompliant behavior. However, if tracking of the procedures and results are in place, teachers will determine if the strategy is effective or not. Finally, including setting event strategies in the intervention plan can impose considerable time, effort, and cost to teachers and specialists.

6

Effects of Noncompliant Behavior

The focus in this chapter is to present strategies for addressing the fourth component of a functional behavioral assessment (FBA)—Effects of Noncompliant Behavior. The central question is, "What strategies should teachers use after noncompliant behavior occurs?" In this sense these strategies are *reactive* because they are implemented *following* the problem behavior. By contrast, the strategies recommended for addressing the previous two components, immediate triggers and setting events (Chapters 4 and 5, respectively), are *proactive* because they are implemented prior to occurrences of noncompliant behavior. At this juncture, a comprehensive plan is now developed comprised of both proactive and reactive measures.

The strategies presented in this chapter are designed to manage the effects or functions of the problem behavior. Essentially, if cooperative behavior is established, then positive or encouraging events follow. If noncompliance occurs, then negative or discouraging events follow. Consequently, the effects of noncompliant behavior are managed by using two groups of strategies. First, strategies are presented for *increasing cooperative behavior,* and second, for *decreasing noncompliant behavior.* These strategies are presented in the last two columns of Table 6.1, Strategies for Effects of Problem Behavior, respectively.

This chapter is divided into two sections in which strategies are described for (1) increasing cooperative behavior and (2) reducing noncompliant behavior. Again, the strategies are listed in alphabetical order and followed by an illustration. Some references are cited for further reading as needed.

Table 6.1   Strategies for Effects of Problem Behavior (See Appendix F: Bank of Strategies for Each FBA Component)

Functional Behavioral Assessment Summary

Setting Events	Immediate Triggers	Problem Behavior	Effects of Problem Behavior

Intervention Plan

Setting Events	Immediate Triggers	Increasing Expected Behavior	Decreasing Problem Behavior

		• Focus on academic success
		• Behavioral contracts
		• Reinforcement
		  ○ Positive
		  ○ Negative
		  ○ Differential reinforcement
		• Shaping
		• Token economies
		• Other
			Tier 1 Strategies
			  • Maintain the flow of instruction
			  • Delayed responding
			  • Extinction
			  • Redirection prompts
			  • Rule restatement
			  • Other
			
			Tier 2 Strategies
			  • Part A: Establishing limits of behavior
			  • Part B: Conducting a debriefing session
			    • Other

STRATEGIES FOR INCREASING   ■
COOPERATIVE BEHAVIOR

Focus on Academic Success

Every effort should be made to ensure that all students are successful with their academics. Given that avoidance of academic tasks and other demand situations are the major reasons for noncompliant behavior, teachers and specialists should take all steps necessary to enable students to be productively engaged and show achievement in their work (Darch & Kame'enui, 2004; Sprick, Garrison, & Howard, 1998; Walker, Colvin, & Ramsey, 1995). Teachers should be ready to provide strong reinforcement for student behaviors that facilitate learning such as making effort, maintaining on-task behavior, work completion, and especially for accuracy in work produced. (*Note:* It is assumed that the student has the skills to do the work, which was addressed in the previous chapter.) An illustration is presented in Box 6.1.

BOX 6.1   ILLUSTRATION OF FOCUS ON ACADEMIC SUCCESS

Cindy was a reluctant oral reader. During oral reading time she would often put her head down, declare she was sick, and periodically refuse to go to the group before reading had even commenced. The teacher had arranged some additional opportunities for her to read aloud to her privately. She then had Cindy practice beforehand the passage she was required to read in the group. Cindy then read reasonably smoothly in the group. The teacher praised her strongly for her reading and arranged for her to have extra time on the computer during the break. She also sent a note home to the parents saying how well she had read and asked them to compliment her.

Behavioral Contract

Behavioral contracts are incentive plans to help students focus on increasing desirable behavior and decreasing problem behavior. Essentially, the plan is a contingency management agreement between the student and the teacher. If the student exhibits compliant or cooperative behavior at a predetermined rate, then the student will have access to privileges or reinforcers. In some contracts, the converse is also added wherein if the student exhibits noncompliant behavior at a predetermined level, then loss of privileges and reinforcers occurs (often called Response Cost). Behavioral contracting has been widely used and is a solid, evidence-based intervention (Hawken & Burrow-Sanchez, 2005; Walker, Colvin, & Ramsey, 1995). The steps in developing a contract need to be carefully developed, clearly communicated to the student, and implemented with adequate supervision. These steps typically involve (1) defining the target behavior to be increased; (2) establishing a criterion for success that is reasonable and attainable; (3) carefully selecting the reinforcers to be used for meeting the terms of the contract; (4) fully communicating the details of the contract with the student and involving the student as much as possible in the development of the contract; (5) developing a simple tracking system so that the student and the teacher readily know if the contract terms have been fulfilled; (6) developing a phasing-out plan that is reasonable; and

(7) formalizing the contract in writing and signed by the teacher and the student. An example of a contract to build cooperative behavior with a student who has a history of noncompliance is presented in Box 6.2.

BOX 6.2   EXAMPLE OF A BEHAVIORAL CONTRACT

My Contract

I _____ (student's name) agree to keep the following rules for math:

1. Follow the teacher directions.
2. Start my work quickly.
3. Keep working.
4. Finish my work in school or at home.
5. Turn in my work on time.

Points: For each rule (1–5) I can earn:

3 points for following the rule all the time.

2 points for following the rule most of the time.

1 point for following the rule only some of the time.

Total points available per Period is 15.

Results: If I earn:

12–15 points: I can spend an extra 15 minutes on the computer (or trade for something else that my teacher has approved). _____

8–11 points: I can spend an extra 10 minutes on the computer (or trade for something else that my teacher has approved). _____

Fewer than 8 points: No extra privileges have been earned.

Start Date: _____

Signed

Student _____   **Teacher** _____

Reinforcement

Reinforcement is defined in terms of its function. Something can be said to be reinforcing if it results in increasing certain behaviors. Positive reinforcement is the contingent delivery of something that is perceived to be desirable for the student and is used to increase occurrences of a target behavior. Negative reinforcement is the contingent removal of something that is perceived to be undesirable by the student and is used to increase occurrences of a target behavior.

Note: Both positive and negative reinforcement are used to *increase* a target behavior.

Positive Reinforcement

This technique is probably the most widely used strategy to increase compliance or cooperative behavior. The keys to using reinforcement successfully are to ensure that (1) the reinforcer is actually positive or desirable for the student; (2) the student needs to exhibit the target behavior at a reasonable standard before the reinforcer is delivered; (3) a menu of reinforcers needs to be available to the student to prevent satiation or boredom; (4) delivery of the reinforcer has to be strictly contingent on the occurrence of the target behavior displayed to an acceptable and reasonable standard; (5) a balance in the kinds of reinforcers between personal (intrinsic), social, and external reinforcers is used; (6) the reinforcers are inexpensive and easy to deliver; and (7) a plan is used to systematically fade the reinforcers used for an individual student to the reinforcers that are used for the whole class (Colvin & Lazar, 1997; Rhode, Jensen, & Reavis, 1992). A range of examples of positive reinforcers is presented in Box 6.3.

BOX 6.3   EXAMPLES OF COMMON POSITIVE REINFORCERS USED IN THE CLASSROOM

Intrinsic

- Teacher helps student focus on accomplishment
- Teacher helps student review goal setting and achievement
- Student self-delivers reinforcement
- Student given opportunity to present accomplishment to class and home

Social

- Teacher praise
- Positive body language (smiles, nods, pat on the back)
- Recognition from class (such as listening or clapping)
- Public display (such as work displayed on notice board)

Tangibles

- Stickers
- Note home
- Ribbons, black belts, and other items teachers gather
- Mystery awards (teacher has a box of goods, and the student does a blind draw)

Physical Activity

- Extra time swimming, walking, or playing
- Opportunity to play favorite game or activity
- Choice activity

Privileges

- Class leader, squad captain
- Distributing and collecting materials or equipment
- Teacher helper
- Running errands
- Schedule adjustments

Class or Group Activities

- Teams (beat the teacher game, good behavior game)
- Goals for the week followed by a group reward (free time, pizza party, TV)
- Class challenges

Negative Reinforcement

Negative reinforcement is often misunderstood and consequently underused in classrooms to increase desirable behavior. The reason it is misunderstood is the combination of the two words—negative and reinforcement. Negative is associated with something undesirable, while reinforcement is often interpreted as something the student enjoys. However, by definition negative reinforcement means that a behavior that is successful in removing something negative or aversive to the student is likely to be repeated, that is, reinforced (Auerbach & Smith, 2005).

Also, there is often confusion between negative reinforcement and punishment. Punishment is the delivery of an undesirable consequence following an unacceptable behavior in order to decrease this behavior. Negative reinforcement, on the other hand, is the removal of something undesirable following the occurrence of behavior resulting in an increase in that behavior. In effect, punishment is a behavior-reduction strategy, while negative reinforcement is a behavior-increasing strategy.

Unfortunately, negative reinforcement has seen its widest application to increasing and maintaining problem behavior. In Chapters 2 and 3, it was noted that the major effects or functions of noncompliant behavior in the classroom were changing, removing, or escaping from a demand situation. In other words, by displaying noncompliant behavior, the student was successful in removing a demand situation (something aversive). The negative reinforcement paradigm has been used for many years to describe the processes for establishing and maintaining aggression, tantrums, and other negative interactions between parents and their children (Patterson & Forgatch, 2005; Patterson, Ray, Shaw, & Cobb, 1969).

In addressing noncompliance, two aspects in using the strategy of negative reinforcement should be addressed: (1) manage the effects and functions of noncompliant behavior that increase and maintain noncompliance (see Extinction in the section Strategies for Reducing Noncompliant Behavior, described later in this chapter), and (2) identify a list of events or activities that have some level of aversion for the student which can be removed or modified contingent on the student displaying compliant and cooperative behavior. See Box 6.4 for a list of common events or activities that teachers use in applying the negative reinforcement strategy.

BOX 6.4   EXAMPLES OF USING NEGATIVE REINFORCEMENT

- Students who obtained high grades in the midterm and had all assignments completed satisfactorily did not have to take the final end-of-term exam.
- Students getting all their work done in school did not have homework.
- A hallway pass was not required of students who kept the class rules for the week.
- Student may withdraw to a quiet area in the room following completion of work.
- Students keeping the rules during break did not have to do cleanup duty.

Differential Reinforcement

Differential reinforcement is an important strategy for addressing non-compliant behavior. Differential reinforcement refers to the delivery of reinforcement contingent on the occurrence of appropriate behavior and withholding of reinforcement in the presence of inappropriate behavior under the same or similar conditions (Burke & Crowder, 2005; Rhode, Jenson, & Reavis, 1992).

Students who exhibit noncompliance at a high rate usually display cooperative behavior at a low rate. Consequently, in order to increase the rate of cooperative behavior for these students, teachers often use differential reinforcement of other behavior (DRO). DRO consists of the reinforcement of any other appropriate behavior that occurs in the *absence of noncompliance* during a set period of time or in the presence of the immediate triggers for noncompliant behavior.

Another important application is called differential reinforcement of incompatible behavior. In this case, the student is reinforced for exhibiting behavior that is contrary to the target problem behavior. Cooperative behavior is incompatible with noncompliant behavior in this situation. Consequently, when the student exhibits compliance or cooperation in a setting where noncompliance often occurs, the student is highly reinforced.

An illustration of the use of differential reinforcement is provided in Box 6.5.

BOX 6.5 ILLUSTRATION OF DIFFERENTIAL REINFORCEMENT

Lily did not like to switch from using the computer to going to her history group. She often pouted, put her head down, and refused to leave. On this occasion when the teacher asked her to finish up on the computer and go to her history group, she finished up the computer activity, pushed her chair in, and went to her group in a reasonable amount of time. The teacher praised her very strongly and told her she could have an extra few minutes on the computer later in the day.

Shaping

Shaping is a common strategy used by teachers, especially for helping students to master new learning. The strategy can also be used to systematically improve student behavior. Shaping is the process of successively reinforcing closer approximations of the target behavior to the criterion or acceptable level of behavior (Maag, 2004). The process involves four steps: (1) obtain a baseline level of performance of the expected behavior or new skill (usually as a rate measure or degree of accuracy); (2) determine successive approximations between the baseline measures and the standard required for mastery or level of acceptable behavior; (3) deliver reinforcement contingent on the student responding at the target level for each successive stage; and (4) deliver the strongest reinforcement when the student reaches the criterion for mastery of the skill, or when the student displays the target acceptable level. This strategy of shaping has been very effective in raising student's skill level in terms of rate of responding and accuracy of performing. The strategy is also helpful in getting students started on a task that they avoid because of the likelihood of failure when there has been a history of failure with these tasks. Shaping can also help reluctant learners "get over the hump" in surmounting perceived difficulties. An illustration of using the shaping technique to improve a student's compliant behavior is described in Box 6.6.

BOX 6.6   ILLUSTRATION OF SHAPING

Juan was very slow in putting his materials away after break time. Sometimes he wouldn't even put them away. The teacher tracked the time he took to clean up after break for a couple of days and also noted the time taken by the other students in the class. These times averaged five minutes and two minutes respectively. The teacher set up with Juan that if he could clean up in four minutes, he could have first choice of the activities for the next break. Juan met this criterion three days in a row. She set a time for him to know when the four minutes were up. The teacher then visited with him, telling him that if he could get the job done in three minutes he could have the same privilege plus a surprise treat. The teacher then moved the criterion to two minutes (the standard for the rest of the class). When Juan made the two-minute mark, the teacher gave him an extra break that day.

Token Economies

Token economies are common strategies used in classrooms to provide incentives to students who have high rates of problem behavior and whose behavior has been resistant to the usual practices used by teachers for managing problem behavior. The process typically involves setting up a plan with a student where the student earns tokens for exhibiting a target behavior, and they may exchange the tokens for reinforcers to be used at another time (Walker, Colvin, & Ramsey, 1995). Token economies are effective because the student can receive immediate feedback and reinforcement, or a token, at high rates following the occurrence of the target behavior. Also, the plan can be developed so that the tokens can be saved, which helps the student exhibit the target behavior over a longer period of time, leading to maintenance of the target behavior. Tokens can be any symbol representing successful performance of behavior specified in the plan such as points, fake money, chips, or stickers. A note of caution: It is important to avoid using items for tokens that the students may use to make unacceptable noise or play with during instruction. The tokens selected should also be age appropriate. The overall steps in developing a token economy plan are (1) specify the target behavior and criterion for correct responding; (2) identify the tokens to be used and how they will be delivered; (3) develop a menu of reinforcement for the particular student and the value in tokens for each item on the menu; (4) clarify the steps for cashing in the tokens and for when the reinforcers may be accessed; and (5) develop a plan to fade the token economy plan once the student is reliably producing the target behavior and is accessing the normal reinforcers in the classroom (Ayllon, 1999). Token economy plans take considerable time and effort for teachers to implement effectively. This strategy is quite effective for students whose noncompliant behavior has been resistant to the less time-consuming strategies. An illustration of a token economy plan is described in Box 6.7 for increasing a student's cooperative behavior in the classroom.

BOX 6.7   ILLUSTRATION OF TOKEN ECONOMY

Loretta's behavior seemed to be getting worse, with high rates of noncompliant behavior in most class periods, and she was displaying more acting-out behavior when she was corrected. The usual strategies were not effective; catching her being compliant and praising her for other expected behavior did not affect the problem behaviors. The teacher decided to establish a token economy plan. He targeted social studies because it was conducted in small cooperative learning groups, as distinct from whole-class instruction. The groups typically worked independently, enabling the teacher to monitor Loretta more easily. The plan was set up with Loretta so that each time she followed a teacher direction, she earned a point, and she earned a point if she was on task when the beeper went off, which was every five minutes during the group activity. The teacher and Loretta made a menu of reinforcers and attached a point value for each item on the list. Loretta was able to cash in the points during the break and purchase her choice of reinforcer from the menu.

Other

Teachers and specialists are strongly encouraged to add strategies to these lists that they have found to be useful with the proviso that these additional selections are appropriate for the particular component of the FBA and have some basis in research to warrant inclusion.

STRATEGIES FOR DECREASING ■
NONCOMPLIANT BEHAVIOR

Even though a solid plan had been developed for addressing the antecedents for the noncompliant behavior, immediate triggers and setting events, and for increasing cooperative behavior, noncompliant behavior may still occur. At least three reasons exist for the persistence of noncompliant behavior: (1) the student may be reinforced for noncompliance in other settings, both at school and at home; (2) the noncompliant behavior may be too firmly established, making it resistant to the proactive measures and a focus on expected behavior; and (3) the noncompliant behavior may still be reinforced in the teacher's classroom, perhaps inadvertently, making the effects of the noncompliant behavior still operative.

The purpose of this section is to describe strategies for implementation in response to the occurrence of problem behavior, specifically noncompliant behavior. These strategies are listed in the column titled Decreasing Problem Behavior in Table 6.1: Strategies for Effects of Problem Behavior. As per the other sections, the strategies vary in the time, effort, and cost requirements of the teacher. The strategies are divided into two tiers. Tier 1 strategies are designed as low-level interventions and may interrupt the noncompliant behavior pattern at an early stage. Tier 2 strategies take more time from the teacher and are designed to be implemented if the student does not respond to Tier 1 strategies or if the student is already engaging in disruptive, serious, noncompliant behavior. Tier 2 strategies are designed as a *bottom line* or *last resort* type of classroom intervention. If these Tier 2 strategies are ineffective in the classroom, the teacher will need additional support to address the behavior, such as back up from the administration and consultation from a specialist. A brief description is provided for each strategy, references for additional reading are cited, and an illustration is provided.

TIER 1 STRATEGIES

Maintain the Flow of Instruction

When students exhibit noncompliance in the classroom, the very first response of the teacher should always be to *maintain the flow of instruction,* unless, of course safety issues or severe disruption are involved (Colvin, 2005a). If a student exhibits noncompliance and instruction is stopped, the student is reinforced by interrupting instruction, securing the attention of the teacher, securing the attention of other students, and by being off task. By contrast, when the student exhibits noncompliance and the teacher maintains the flow of instruction, the noncompliant behavior is not reinforced because nothing changes. There are no *immediate* effects of the noncompliant behavior. If the student begins to cooperate, the teacher would briefly acknowledge the student. If the student did not cooperate, additional steps would be taken to address the noncompliant behavior.

BOX 6.8   ILLUSTRATION FOR MAINTAINING THE FLOW OF INSTRUCTION AS FIRST RESPONSE

The teacher was explaining the relationship between the invasion of Hawaii and the war in Europe against Germany. He directed the class to read the first paragraph of their text on page 84. Steffan mumbled that he was not interested in reading that paragraph and would sooner read the sports section of the paper. The teacher continued, without pausing, to tell the class what to look for in the paragraph. He acknowledged the class for paying attention and gestured to Steffan to begin reading. Steffan began to read, the teacher quietly acknowledged him, and then told the class that they had a couple more minutes to finish the reading.

Delayed Responding

This strategy is sometimes called planned ignoring. The teacher notices the noncompliant behavior of the student but does not respond in any way to this student. The teacher simply continues with instruction as if nothing had happened and acknowledges students who are cooperating. The idea is that if the student wants attention, then the way to get it is to cooperate and take part in the lesson. However, if the student persists with noncompliance, then additional, more direct steps would be taken. An illustration is provided in Box 6.9.

> **BOX 6.9   ILLUSTRATION FOR DELAYED RESPONDING**
>
> The teacher announces to the class that writing time is over and asks them to put their materials away and get ready for physical education (PE). The class begins to put their material away except for Henri, who keeps writing in his book while muttering that he doesn't like PE. The teacher, while noticing Henri's response, ignores him and moves around the class, acknowledging the students who are putting away their materials and complimenting the class on the good writing period.

Extinction

Extinction is the generic term used to describe the process for discontinuing or withholding the reinforcers that are maintaining a behavior. In this sense, the previous two strategies, maintaining the flow of instruction and delayed responding, are *extinction strategies* because they are designed to withhold immediate attention following noncompliant behavior. In general, noncompliant behavior is reinforced by securing attention and by avoidance or escape from a required task (see Chapter 3). By using extinction strategies, the teacher takes measures to teach the student that (1) attention will not be obtained through noncompliance but, rather, will be obtained through cooperation, and (2) noncompliant behavior will not be successful in modifying, removing, or escaping from a task. Although the extinction process is logically sound, it is difficult to implement consistently. The reasons are that (1) the teacher may have reflexive responses to noncompliant behavior, causing the noncompliance to be reinforced inadvertently; (2) the student may be reinforced for noncompliant behavior in other settings in the school or at home; (3) other students may be reinforcing the students' behavior by providing attention and support; (4) teachers often permit low levels of noncompliance to occur, that is, not to respond immediately, in order for the extinction process to take effect; and (5) students may escalate their behavior once they perceive that their usual level of noncompliant behavior is not working (known as an extinction burst), which forces the teacher to respond to this high level of problem behavior (Lane, 2005). However, despite these challenges, teachers and specialists are highly encouraged to use extinction strategies to address noncompliant behavior, otherwise the problem behavior may persist. An illustration of an extinction strategy is described in Box 6.10.

> **BOX 6.10   ILLUSTRATION FOR EXTINCTION STRATEGY**
>
> The history teacher enjoyed having discussion time with his class but found the students were talking out a lot, interrupting each other, and did not seem to be listening to each other. To change the situation, he introduced a rule that you must put up your hand if you had something to say. He told the class he appreciated them wanting to make their comments, but the discussions had become too unruly. By and large the class followed this direction except for Angela. She kept calling out her comments and would not put up her
>
> *(Continued)*

(Continued)

hand. Reminders did not seem to help Angela raise her hand. The teacher decided to put Angela's talking-out on extinction. He reminded the class of the need to put up their hand to talk and only called on those who raised their hand. When Angela talked out the teacher very quickly went to another student whose hand was raised and said, "Yes, Bobbi, thanks for raising your hand." The teacher noted that very shortly after this exchange, Angela shouted her comment. The teacher presumed he was dealing with an extinction burst and proceeded in the same way by calling on another student. On another occasion Angela raised her hand, and the teacher called on her immediately, responded positively to her comment, and prompted the class to respond to her comments.

Redirection Prompts

When students who exhibit noncompliance in the classroom do not respond to the lowest level of intervention, extinction, the next level involves redirection prompts. These prompts are designed to assist the student to focus on the request provided by the teacher with *minimum attention* given to the student (Colvin & Lazar, 1997; Walker, Colvin, & Ramsey, 1995). By contrast with the extinction strategies, attention is provided directly, albeit briefly, to the student who is displaying noncompliance. The redirection prompts are typically gestures or a brief verbal response. The term *redirection* is used because the goal of the prompt is to shift the student from noncompliance to cooperation. The student is acknowledged briefly if cooperation ensues. An illustration is provided in Box 6.11.

BOX 6.11   ILLUSTRATION FOR REDIRECTION PROMPTING

The students are on a break, and the teacher announces that the break is over and requests that they move to their desks and get ready for math. The class responds as requested, except for Michelle, who begins to wander the room. The teacher acknowledges the students who have moved to their desk and are ready for math. Michelle is still wandering the room. The teacher says, quietly but loud enough for Michelle to hear, "Michelle, math time," and points to her desk. Michelle circles a little more and goes to her desk. The teacher catches her eye, smiles, gives her a nod, and then begins the math lesson.

Rule Restatement

For some students redirection prompts are not direct enough. These students need a clearer communication of what has been requested to assist them in following directions. In these cases, it is helpful to directly secure the student's attention and restate the rule or expectation. The assumption is that the rule or expectation has been established and the majority of the class is cooperating. However, some students need more direction to help them disengage from the off-task or noncompliant behavior. Two steps are recommended in using this strategy: (1) directly secure student's attention and (2) restate the rule in a positive yet firm tone. Again, if the student does not cooperate, additional steps need to be taken such as the Tier 2 strategies. See Box 6.12 for an illustration for Rule Restatement.

BOX 6.12   ILLUSTRATION FOR RULE RESTATEMENT

The students are finishing up a project. When they finish, they are expected to put their project in the teacher's basket, select a book from the shelf, and read quietly. Gerald moved to the book shelf and started perusing the books. The teacher acknowledges the students who had turned in their projects and had begun their reading. Gerald persisted with thumbing through books on the bookshelf. The teacher approached him directly and said, "Gerald, look here please." Gerald looked at the teacher. The teacher said, "Good. Listen, you've been asked to turn in your project and then get a book. So please, go back to your desk and turn in your project, then you may come back here and get a book." Gerald hesitated, put the book back and went to his desk. The teacher caught him as he was heading to the shelf after turning in his work and said, "There you go. Thanks."

Other

Teachers and specialists are strongly encouraged to add strategies to these lists that they have found to be useful with the proviso that these additional selections are appropriate for the particular component of the FBA and have some basis in research to warrant inclusion.

TIER 2 INTERVENTIONS: ADDRESSING PERSISTENT AND SERIOUS NONCOMPLIANCE ■

Reasonable questions from teachers highly likely to arise at this point are as follows:

- "What if you have tried the proactive strategies for addressing antecedents, worked hard to increase cooperative behavior, and have tried planned ignoring and other extinction strategies and the student still persists with noncompliant behavior?"
- "Is there a bottom line here?"
- "When is enough enough?"
- "What if the behavior is very serious and disruptive right from the start? I just can't ignore that, right?"

Clearly, teachers need an intervention designed for addressing noncompliant behavior that is resistant to the strategies described so far in this book, and for noncompliant behavior that begins with serious disruption. However, when teachers address forms of noncompliance, there is always the chance that the student may escalate further to more disruptive, and perhaps unsafe behavior (Colvin, 1999; Colvin, 2004). Consequently, strategies used for this level of behavior, Tier 2, have a double goal of securing cooperation from the student and, at the same time, avoiding escalating the student behavior. To achieve these goals, there are two parts to this intervention: (1) establishing limits of behavior and (2) conducting a debriefing session.

Part A: Establishing Limits of Behavior

This procedure is designed to provide clear and unambiguous communication to the student that cooperation is expected or there will be consequences. In addition, this communication has to be presented in a way that will not escalate the student's behavior. The procedure has three steps: (1) establish initial setup; (2) present the choices as a decision; and (3) follow through based on the student's decision.

Step 1: Establish Initial Setup

This strategy is more effective when the procedures are described to the students at the start of the school year. In this way there are no surprises for the students, and the teachers do not have to think quickly on their feet when the problem behavior may be accelerating. There are two parts to setting up the procedures: (1) rehearse the steps with the class and (2) establish a short list of negative consequences.

Rehearse the Steps with the Class. Early in the school year, preferably during the first week of class, the teacher should go over these procedures when other organizational items are explained. This information would be included as part of the classroom management system used by the teacher.

Establish a Short List of Negative Consequences. The purpose of using negative consequences is to communicate to the students that there are limits to behavior that can be accepted in the classroom. In other words, negative consequences may be delivered when students do not cooperate with the classroom expectations and rules. Consequences typically used by classroom teachers are as follows:

- Loss of privileges (such as computer time, free time, free choice time)
- Loss of recess or breaks
- Office referral
- Detention
- Loss of points
- Loss of something earned
- Parent call
- Time-out
- Removal to another room

Step 2: Present the Choices as a Decision

The intent of this step is to *direct the focus* of the interaction with the student to expected behavior. The student is trying to engage the teacher through noncompliance. However, the teacher does not respond directly to the noncompliant behavior (which the student expects). Rather, the teacher focuses on the student making a choice between following the expected behavior and receiving a negative consequence for noncompliance.

It is helpful for the teacher to use a simple formula, such as the following:

- Present the *expected behavior* and the *negative consequence* as a decision for the student to make.
- Allow some time for the student to decide (usually a minute or so).
- Withdraw from the student, attend to other students, or engage in some other task.

Two illustrations of this procedure are presented in Box 6.13.

BOX 6.13 **ILLUSTRATIONS OF TEACHER PRESENTING DECISION TO NONCOMPLIANT STUDENT**

Note: In each of these examples the teacher has tried other strategies described earlier in this book to elicit student cooperation.

Example 1: Sophia refuses to clean up her area after free choice time. The teacher secures her attention and says to her, "Sophia, you are asked to put things away in your area (*expectation*), otherwise you will have to do it at recess (*negative consequence*). You have a minute or so to decide (*decision*)." The teacher leaves Sophia and goes to other students (*teacher withdraws*).

Example 2: Austen is wandering the room, chatting to other students, reading the bulletin board, and disrupting other students. The teacher tells him that he needs to be at his desk doing his math. He looks the teacher in the eye and says, "No way. You can't make me." The teacher pauses, compliments another student who is nearby and on task, looks at Austen and says, "Austen, this has gone too far. You are asked to go to your desk and start on your math (*expectation*), or I will have to send you to the office for insubordination (*negative consequence*). You have a few seconds to decide (*decision*)." The teacher then moves around the room checking the class's work (*teacher withdraws*).

Step 3: Follow Through Based on the Student's Decision

The follow-through steps taken by the teacher are dependent on whether the student decided to follow the expected behavior or to maintain noncompliant behavior. There are three common possible outcomes for the student's decision. The student may decide to (1) exhibit the expected behavior; (2) maintain the noncompliant behavior; or (3) maintain the problem behavior, then belatedly switch to the expected behavior. Each of these possibilities is addressed.

Student Exhibits Expected Behavior. If the student decides to exhibit the expected behavior, acknowledge the choice *briefly*, and continue with the lesson or activity. It is very important to be brief and low key in acknowledging the student in this situation because the student may still be agitated or may need to save face in front of other students. Return to the student shortly and interact briefly and momentarily acknowledge the student's on-task behavior with a comment such as, "Thanks for getting started."

Student Maintains Noncompliant Behavior. If the student does not choose the expected behavior, that is, decides to maintain the noncompliant behavior, the teacher delivers the negative consequence. The language used by the teacher is important in order to clearly communicate ownership of the decision to the student. For example, "John, you are telling me you have chosen to do your work during recess. Okay, that's what we will do." In this way, the teacher is not only clarifying the choice that the student has made, but the language used puts the responsibility of the decision with the student. In effect, the student is accountable and responsible for the consequence that is delivered.

Student Maintains Noncompliance, Then Belatedly Switches to the Expected Behavior. Once students become familiar with the teacher's follow-through procedure, it is common for some of them to try a delayed, manipulative tactic. They maintain the noncompliant behavior and after the teacher tells them that they have chosen the negative consequence, they will then switch to the expected behavior. The teacher really needs to *follow through* with the negative consequence, at least to some extent, in order to establish limits. Otherwise, students will learn that it is acceptable to show noncompliance as long as they eventually switch to cooperation. Basically, they are testing limits. It might be reasonable to deliver just part of the negative consequence on the basis that the student did eventually cooperate. However, the teacher should visit with the student at some point later to clarify the procedures with the student, especially the criterion for an acceptable and timely response.

Part B: Conducting a Debriefing Session

The purpose of the debriefing session is to *problem-solve* and prepare students so they will be better equipped to exhibit cooperative behavior the next time a similar situation arises. There are five steps in conducting a debriefing process: (1) select a time to meet with the student; (2) clarify the purpose of the meeting; (3) identify the sequence of events for the noncompliant incident; (4) pinpoint decision moments during the sequence of events; and (5) identify acceptable decision options for future situations (Colvin, 2004; Sugai & Colvin, 1997).

Step 1: Select a Time to Meet With the Student

Because the debriefing session is designed to be supportive and constructive, best results are obtained when the meeting occurs after any negative consequences have been delivered and after the student is back on track in the classroom. In this way, the student is more likely to cooperate and participate in the meeting and less likely to perceive the debriefing session as part of the negative consequences.

Step 2: Clarify the Purpose of the Debriefing Session

The teacher tries to ensure that the student understands the meeting has been called to help him or her become more successful in class. The teacher makes every effort to make the meeting a positive, problem-solving, and supportive event, resulting in the student having a firm plan for handling future similar problem situations.

Step 3: Identify the Sequence of Events for the Noncompliant Incident

Here the teacher walks the student through the series of events leading up to the noncompliance; what the student actually exhibited as noncompliant behavior; the effects of the noncompliant behavior on the classroom; and, finally, the consequences for the noncompliant behavior. These issues are identified and reviewed in a calm, nonjudgmental, and matter-of-fact manner.

Step 4: Pinpoint Decision Moments During the Sequence of Events

This step involves helping the student see the relationship between his or her decisions and subsequent events and to set the stage for making better decisions in the future. The major emphasis here is to help students understand that they are in *control* of their behavior and subsequent events. The relationship between their decisions and these events are clarified and emphasized.

Step 5: Identify Acceptable Decision Options for Future Situations

The intent of this final step is to prepare the students for how they might handle future events differently so that incidents are prevented and expected behavior is more likely to occur. The basic question to be addressed with the student is, "What else could you have done that would be acceptable?" The answer generally lies with the decisions and subsequent behavior exhibited by other students in the class. It is best to have the student actually commit to making *good* choices in the future and to rehearse the situation with an emphasis on concrete alternative behaviors to be followed in future.

An illustration of the debriefing process is described in Box 6.14.

B O X   6.14   ILLUSTRATION FOR DEBRIEFING PROCESS

Simone had been sent to the office for shouting at the teacher, refusing to do her work, and wandering the classroom disrupting other students. The teacher had tried several steps to help Simone show more cooperation in class and to follow directions. This was the first time she had been sent to the office.

After about 30 minutes, she returned to class and the teacher prompted her to join her group for science. Simone started out slowly and then entered quite fully into the class activities. The teacher mentioned to her privately that she needed to see her after the break. At the end of the break, the class was directed to work independently on their reports, and the teacher beckoned Simone to visit at the teacher's desk. The teacher pointed out that she wanted to have a few words to examine the incident earlier and to see what can be changed so it won't happen again, noting that Simone can be more successful just like she has been in the group just now. She had Simone begin the discussion with where she started to resist reading the science text on volcanoes and identified that she wouldn't accept any help and stopped working altogether. When she was reminded to keep working, she left her seat and wandered the room, beginning to disrupt other students. When she was given a warning to take her seat, she blew up, shouting at the teacher, and then she was sent to the office. The teacher asked her to examine the decisions she made, including to stop working, to leave her seat, to disrupt other students,

(Continued)

(Continued)

and finally to begin shouting at the teacher. Simone indicated that reading science is hard, and she was having a bad day anyway. The teacher suggested that she might ask for help and that she would check on her work a little more often. They chatted a little about some options for when she is upset over something—to ask for some space, to tough it out, or go to another place in the room. Simone agreed to ask for help and to take a quiet place in the room when she needs some space. The teacher thanked her for her cooperation, encouraged her to do her best, and asked her if she was up to making a start on the report at her desk.

Other

Teachers and specialists are strongly encouraged to add strategies to these lists that they have found to be useful with the proviso that these additional selections are appropriate for the particular component of the FBA and have some basis in research to warrant inclusion.

■ CHAPTER SUMMARY

Noncompliant behavior has proven to be elusive for educators to effectively change for a number of reasons. One major reason for the behavior to be resistant to many of the normal practices in the classroom is that the *effects of the noncompliant behavior* are quite powerful in maintaining the behavior. Specifically, noncompliant behavior can be very effective in avoiding or escaping from a demand situation. In addition, the behavior can be very effective in obtaining teacher attention. Unfortunately, there are no quick solutions for eliminating the reinforcing effects of noncompliant behavior in the classroom. However, there are well-established strategies that teachers and specialists can use to systematically increase cooperative behavior and reduce noncompliance. In some cases, these strategies, in conjunction with the proactive approaches described in Chapters 4 and 5, and earlier in Chapter 6, are not strong enough to change the noncompliant behavior. In these events, a "bottom-line" procedure needs to be in place that is designed to communicate to the student that the noncompliance needs to cease or negative consequences will follow. Specific steps were described for this procedure to help ensure that the expected behavior of cooperation is emphasized and that the consequences for noncompliance are presented in a way to avoid further escalation. At this juncture, if noncompliant behavior still persists, there would be the need to obtain administrative support or backup and perhaps consultation from a specialist or behavior support team.

7

Putting It All Together

At this juncture, a teacher may make the comment that options for behavioral interventions for addressing noncompliant behavior are just too overwhelming. The implication is that it is not really possible to engage in all of these interventions that have been identified in Chapters 4, 5, and 6 for a student or a few students and still be expected to provide instruction and management for the rest of the class. These comments make the point very clearly, and reasonably, that there needs to be a systematic plan for determining which functional behavioral assessment (FBA) components to address, which strategies to select, how to construct a plan, and how to modify a plan as needed in ways that still permit the proper management and instruction of the rest of the class.

The purpose of this chapter is to establish guidelines for educators in developing an intervention plan that is likely to be *effective* for the student and *manageable* for the teacher. The basic approach will be to identify key variables involved in the design and implementation of a plan, and then to select strategies that are appropriate for addressing these variables. There are four main parts to this chapter: (1) identification of the major variables for developing intervention plans; (2) guidelines for developing intervention plans; (3) illustrations of intervention plans; and (4) application to earlier case studies.

IDENTIFICATION OF MAJOR VARIABLES FOR DEVELOPING AN INTERVENTION PLAN

A number of research and evidence-based strategies have been identified for each component of an FBA. However, the effectiveness of the strategy may be limited to certain conditions in the classroom that may not be replicated in other settings. For example, one classroom may have a very competent teacher assistant, whereas another may not have an assistant. Another classroom may have strong administrative support from the principal, whereas in another classroom the teacher is basically without such support. It is very important when selecting which strategies to use in an intervention plan to carefully consider key variables operating in the school and classroom. The following factors should be carefully considered before determining which strategies to use in the intervention plan.

Accurate Functional Behavioral Assessment

A major premise of this book is that an accurate FBA has been conducted. Sometimes the teacher may not have adequate training on how to conduct these assessments or interpret them, or have time to conduct one. In these cases, teachers will either need to obtain more training or elicit assistance of someone who is trained, such as a district specialist or a behavior support team member.

Emphasis on Positive Approaches

A fundamental priority in this book is to use positive approaches for addressing noncompliant behavior. This means the emphasis in designing a plan is to select strategies more likely to increase the behaviors that are expected versus focusing on strategies to reduce problem behavior. Granted, both strategies are needed. The issue is balance, and emphasis needs to be toward use of the strategies designed to build desirable behaviors that will assist students in being successful in the classroom.

Emphasis on Proactive Approaches

Proactive approaches, as the name suggests, are implemented before the student has the opportunity to exhibit noncompliant behavior. By contrast, reactive approaches, typically punitive measures, are implemented after the student has engaged in noncompliant behavior. Again, both approaches are necessary and have important functions. However, the emphasis needs to be on utilizing proactive measures.

A great strength in using an FBA is that critical information is obtained on the Immediate Triggers and Setting Events, which can be directly manipulated by using a variety of strategies *before* the student has an opportunity to exhibit noncompliance. By using proactive strategies, the teacher is actually "stacking the deck" for the student to exhibit cooperative and appropriate behavior.

Teacher Constraints

A key for determining which strategies to use in a classroom is to carefully evaluate the constraints operating in any given classroom. One constraint is the level of support a teacher may have. Typical supports include district personnel, such as behavior specialists or consultants; other building and district support staff, including school psychologists, counselors and social workers; and outside community resources, which may involve other agencies, grants, or college resources.

A second constraint centers on the composition of the class. One classroom may have only one or two students who exhibit challenging behavior, while other classrooms may have several students who need fairly intensive support plans. Clearly, a teacher cannot implement strategies that are time consuming on an individual basis to several students at the same time. The choice of strategies will be influenced by the number of students needing assistance.

A third constraint relates to the configuration of the classroom itself. Obviously if the room is small and crowded, it becomes difficult to set up various stations, time-out areas, free-choice areas, and so on. The strategies used must be able to be implemented and not compromised by the limitations of the classroom size, location, and arrangement.

Finally, a key to success in using most strategies is the quality of administrative support provided to the teacher by the principal or assistant principal. This component is most essential when a teacher is developing plans for the students who display serious and challenging noncompliant behavior.

Cost, Time, and Effort

The strategies presented in this book vary considerably in the cost, time, and effort to implement. Given that a teacher has multiple responsibilities in a classroom, it makes sense to begin an intervention plan with the least intrusive strategies. If the students do not respond to this level of intervention, then move to more intrusive and intensive strategies.

Personal Preferences

A major advantage in using an FBA approach for addressing noncompliant behavior is that a number of strategies can be generated to address information arising from this assessment. Some of these strategies may be more preferable to teachers than others. Moreover, teachers and specialists may know and use effectively strategies not included on the lists provided in this book. The central issue is that whatever strategies are used, there is a clear rationale and evidence base for the selection, and that the strategies are designed to address a particular component of the FBA.

Progress Monitoring

Once the assessment steps have been undertaken and an intervention plan has been developed and implemented, it is particularly important to monitor the progress of the plan. Typically, data need to be collected and reviewed in an ongoing manner. Given teachers have much to deal with during their day, data collection and review needs to be as simple and least time consuming as possible. Data collected should reflect the original issues of concern such as the frequency of office referrals and amount of disruption for the more intense behaviors. If the noncompliance occurs at specific times, locations, or tasks, frequency or sampling data could be collected. Finally, school functioning data could also be collected such as improvement in work completion, grades, attendance, and participation in class activities.

Data not only provide information on progress, but also help to provide a basis for making decisions. For example, if the student is making solid progress, decisions can be made to begin fading the intervention. Conversely, if the student is not making satisfactory progress, the intervention may need to be revised and more supports added to the plans. Progress monitoring is *the key* to evaluating plans and for making appropriate program decisions.

Response to Previous Interventions

Recently, Response to Intervention (RtI) has become an important practice in providing services through the Individuals with Disabilities Education Act (IDEA 2004; Fuchs & Deshler, 2007). The basic tenet of RtI has been a long-standing practice in behavioral literature in which the teacher takes ongoing data to check if the student is gaining mastery of the skill being taught and if there are measureable changes in a behavior being targeted (Hale, 2006). If the intervention is not working, according to the data, adjustments are made to the instruction or intervention. In the case of addressing noncompliant behavior in the classroom, the teacher selects strategies and tracks the student's level of cooperation. If the student is making progress, the intervention plan is maintained, and if not, the strategies may be adjusted or replaced.

Level of Behavioral Intensity

Behavioral intensity is a subjective yet very important variable for developing an intervention plan to address noncompliant behavior. Intensity refers to the extent to which the behavior impacts the classroom. If the behavior significantly disrupts classroom instruction so that instruction cannot continue, or if there is concern for the safety of students and staff, then the behavior is deemed *very intense*. These behaviors require a comprehensive plan that takes time, effort, cost, and extensive coordination (Tier 2 strategies). However, the behavior of a student who exhibits mild resistance to directions and does not disrupt the classroom or impact other students in any way would be considered *low intensity*. These behaviors would require selecting simpler interventions carried out just by the teacher (Tier 1 strategies).

Incidence or Frequency of the Noncompliant Behavior

Another determining variable for the selection of strategies is simply how often the behavior occurs. Typically, low-frequency or low-incidence behaviors require simpler interventions than high-incidence behaviors (unless, of course, the behavior has high intensity). A low-intensity behavior, in itself, may not be disruptive, but if it becomes high frequency, it can be wearing and challenging to the teacher and interfere with the student's progress. Consequently, high-frequency behavior typically requires more comprehensive or Tier 2 levels of interventions.

GUIDELINES FOR DEVELOPING ■
AN INTERVENTION PLAN

Once the teacher, specialist, or behavior support team has evaluated the particular relevance of the variables identified above, the next step is to develop an intervention plan to target the student's noncompliant behavior. A relatively simple approach to developing a plan is to organize the details of the strategies around two determining measures—level of *intensity* and level of *incidence*. In Table 7.1, four key groups of interventions are listed based on the interaction between measures of low and high incidence and low and high intensity: (1) low incidence and low intensity (Level 1 Interventions); (2) high incidence and low intensity (Level 2 Interventions); (3) low incidence high intensity (Level 3 Interventions); and (4) high incidence high intensity (Level 4 Interventions).

The approach is to select strategies from the table provided in Part II, Bank of Strategies for Each FBA Component, for each of these levels of intervention. For Level 1 Interventions, the least intrusive and least time-consuming strategies are selected. Levels 2–4 Interventions require increasing time, effort, cost, and degree of complexity, as the behavior becomes more serious with respect to incidence and intensity.

Level 1 Intervention: Low Incidence and Low Intensity

The assumption here is the noncompliant behavior is not very serious, but needs to be addressed so that it does not become more serious and show increases in frequency and intensity. For this level of behavior, an FBA is still recommended; however, the teacher may focus primarily on the Immediate Triggers and the Effects of the Noncompliant Behavior.

Note: For the more serious levels of noncompliant behavior, Levels 3 and 4, Setting Events would be examined. In designing a plan for Level 1 Intervention, the teacher is encouraged to select strategies from Table 7.2 with an emphasis on the FBA components for addressing the Immediate Triggers and Increasing Expected Behavior *(cooperation and compliance)*. Typically Tier 1 strategies are selected.

Level 2 Intervention: High Frequency and Low Intensity

This level of intervention is needed for those students who display noncompliance quite frequently, but the behavior itself does not interfere with other students and has limited impact on the classroom. However,

Table 7.1   Relationship Between Incidence, Intensity, and Level of Intervention

	Low Incidence	*High Incidence*
Low intensity	Level 1 Intervention	Level 2 Intervention
High intensity	Level 3 Intervention	Level 4 Intervention

Table 7.2 Strategies for Designing a Level 1 Intervention Plan (See Appendix F: Bank of Strategies for Each FBA Component)

Functional Behavioral Assessment Summary

Setting Events	Immediate Triggers	Problem Behavior	Effects of Problem Behavior

Intervention Plan

Setting Events	Immediate Triggers	Increasing Expected Behavior	Decreasing Problem Behavior

	Tier 1 Strategies
	• Active supervision
	• Behavioral momentum
	• Defusing techniques
	• Pacing
	• Prompting
	• Opportunities to respond
	• Other
		• Focus on academic success
		• Reinforcement
		  ○ Positive
		  ○ Differential reinforcement
		• Other
			Tier 1 Strategies
			• Maintain the flow of instruction
			• Delayed responding
			• Extinction
			• Redirection prompts
			• Other

this level of behavior can become a problem for the teacher as time and attention are taken away from other students. In addition, frequent low-level noncompliance will limit the individual student's success in class, which can set the stage for more serious problem behavior in the future. Clearly, the behavior needs to be addressed. The strategies selected in these cases need to be more comprehensive and time consuming, and usually need to involve some Tier 2 selections. Recommended selections for this level are presented in Table 7.3.

Level 3 Intervention: Low Incidence and High Intensity

This level of behavior should be a red flag to educators—noncompliant behavior that is serious but not very frequent. The issue is that the behavior may become more frequent, creating a serious and challenging concern. Moreover, if unchecked, this behavior pattern could have very harmful effects on the student's success in school and in later life. At this juncture, the teacher, specialist, or behavior support team would be advised to invest more time and effort into designing a more comprehensive intervention plan to include strategies from the FBA component, Setting Events, and to introduce the Tier 2 strategy for establishing limits from the Decreasing Problem Behavior component. The pool for recommended strategies is listed in Table 7.4.

Level 4: High Incidence and High Intensity

This is the worst-case scenario, where the student displays the most serious level of noncompliant behavior at a high rate. For this most challenging class of noncompliance, educators need to develop a comprehensive and all-inclusive intervention plan drawing on all the resources available. The main difference in designing a plan for a Level 4 Intervention, compared with a Level 3 Intervention, is the recommended inclusion of strategies for including parents and the wraparound process. In effect, the teacher, specialist, or behavior support team needs to draw from the full bank of strategies listed in Table 7.5.

ILLUSTRATIONS OF INTERVENTION PLANS ∎

A classroom illustration is provided for each level of intervention described in the previous section. Four parts are described in each illustration: (1) initial concern, (2) FBA, (3) intervention plan, and (4) table of FBA Summary and Intervention Plan.

Level 1 Interventions: Illustration for Low-Incidence and Low-Intensity Noncompliance

Initial Concern

The teacher notices that Kayla is showing more resistance in following directions. She starts to pout, puts her head down, and makes excuses why she cannot do what is asked of her. The teacher decides that it is time to

Table 7.3 Strategies for Designing a Level 2 Intervention Plan (See Appendix F: Bank of Strategies for Each FBA Component)

Functional Behavioral Assessment Summary			
Setting Events	*Immediate Triggers*	*Problem Behavior*	*Effects of Problem Behavior*

Intervention Plan			
Setting Events	*Immediate Triggers*	*Increasing Expected Behavior*	*Decreasing Problem Behavior*

	Tier 1 Strategies
	• Active supervision
	• Behavioral momentum
	• Defusing techniques
	• Pacing
	• Prompting
	• Opportunities to respond
	• Other
	
	Tier 2 Strategies
	• Behavior rehearsal
	• Context modification
	• Fading
	• Minimizing errors
	• Precorrection
	• Task interspersal
	• Stimulus control
	• Other
		• Focus on academic success
		• Behavioral contracts
		• Reinforcement
		  ○ Positive
		  ○ Negative
		  ○ Differential reinforcement
		• Shaping
		• Token economies
		• Other
			Tier 1 Strategies
			• Maintain the flow of instruction
			• Delayed responding
			• Extinction
			• Redirection prompts
			• Rule restatement
			• Other

Table 7.4 Strategies for Designing a Level 3 Intervention Plan (See Appendix F: Bank of Strategies for Each FBA Component)

Functional Behavioral Assessment Summary

Setting Events	Immediate Triggers	Problem Behavior	Effects of Problem Behavior

Intervention Plan

Setting Events	Immediate Triggers	Increasing Expected Behavior	Decreasing Problem Behavior

• Academic assessment and instructional decision making
• Anger management
• Conflict resolution
• Curriculum intervention
• Instructional delivery
• Individual behavior instruction plan
• Parent involvement
• Teacher-student relationship
• Self-management skills
• Social skills instruction
• Other
	Tier 1 Strategies
	• Active supervision
	• Behavioral momentum
	• Defusing techniques
	• Pacing
	• Prompting
	• Opportunities to respond
	• Other
	
	Tier 2 Strategies
	• Behavior rehearsal
	• Context modification
	• Fading
	• Minimizing errors
	• Precorrection
	• Task interspersal
	• Stimulus control
	• Other
		• Focus on academic success
		• Behavioral contracts
		• Reinforcement
		  ○ Positive
		  ○ Negative
		  ○ Differential Reinforcement
		• Shaping
		• Token economies
		• Other
			Tier 1 Strategies
			• Maintain the flow of instruction
			• Delayed responding
			• Extinction
			• Redirection prompts
			• Rule restatement
			• Other
			
			Tier 2 Strategies
			• Part A: Establishing limits of behavior
			• Part B: Conducting a debriefing session
			• Other

Table 7.5   Strategies for Designing a Level 4 Intervention Plan (See Appendix F: Bank of Strategies for Each FBA Component)

Functional Behavioral Assessment Summary

Setting Events	Immediate Triggers	Problem Behavior	Effects of Problem Behavior

Intervention Plan

Setting Events	Immediate Triggers	Increasing Expected Behavior	Decreasing Problem Behavior

• Academic assessment and instructional decision making
• Anger management
• Conflict resolution
• Curriculum intervention
• Instructional delivery
• Individual behavior instruction plan
• Parent involvement
• Teacher-student relationship
• Self-management skills
• Social skills instruction
• Wraparound process
• Other
	Tier 1 Strategies
	• Active supervision
	• Behavioral momentum
	• Defusing techniques
	• Pacing
	• Prompting
	• Opportunities to respond
	• Other
	
	Tier 2 Strategies
	• Behavior rehearsal
	• Context modification
	• Fading
	• Minimizing errors
	• Precorrection
	• Task interspersal
	• Stimulus control
	• Other
		• Focus on academic success
		• Behavioral contracts
		• Reinforcement
		  ○ Positive
		  ○ Negative
		  ○ Differential Reinforcement
		• Shaping
		• Token economies
		• Other
			Tier 1 Strategies
			• Maintain the flow of instruction
			• Delayed responding
			• Extinction
			• Redirection prompts
			• Rule restatement
			• Other
			
			Tier 2 Strategies
			• Part A: Establishing limits of behavior
			• Part B: Conducting a debriefing session
			• Other

address the problem so as to prevent it going further and to make the student more successful in school.

Functional Behavioral Assessment

Because the behavior was just emerging and infrequent, the teacher decided to conduct an abbreviated functional assessment. Specifically, the teacher examined where and when the noncompliant behavior occurred, Immediate Triggers, and what happened following the noncompliant behavior, Effects of Problem Behavior. It was observed that while noncompliance occurred throughout the day, most incidents occurred following the transition from reading to math. Reading was usually conducted in small groups, and math began as independent work. The teacher concluded also that the noncompliant behavior had the effect of securing more attention from the teacher and in delaying work on math. The teacher had reliable information that the student was able to do the math.

Intervention Plan

The teacher selected *precorrection* and *behavioral momentum* from strategies for the Immediate Triggers component of the FBA list. Just before the switch from reading to math, the teacher made contact with the student, praised her for some aspect of the reading class, mentioned that math would be on shortly, and encouraged her to get started quickly (precorrection). The teacher gave her a couple of directions at the end of reading, which Kayla followed, and prompted her to head to her desk and get out her math book, which she did. The teacher praised her for cooperation and directed her to start the first problem in math and gave her more praise for cooperating (behavioral momentum and positive reinforcement). The teacher also selected *differential reinforcement* from the list of Effects of Problem Behavior of the FBA list. The teacher acknowledged Kayla when she was on task with her math and ignored her when she was not working (differential reinforcement). Progress was tracked by noting whether Kayla moved from reading to math reasonably quickly and began work on the math problems as per the rest of the class. The plan depicting FBA summary and strategy selections is presented in Table 7.6, FBA Summary and Intervention Plan, Level 1 Illustration.

Level 2 Interventions: Illustration for High-Incidence and Low-Intensity Noncompliance

Initial Concern

The teacher was puzzled by Toby's noncompliant behavior. Sometimes he was very cooperative and engaged in the class activities, and other times he would become noncompliant. He would often wander the room, mumbling to himself, and refuse to follow any directions to sit down and begin what the other students were doing. When he was directed to go to his desk or to begin working on what the other students were engaged in, he would walk the room and mumble to himself. He did not disrupt the class or try to engage other students. However, the behavior took teacher time and interrupted the student's learning time.

Table 7.6   FBA Summary and Intervention Plan, Level 1 Illustration (See Appendix A: FBA Summary and Intervention Plan)

Functional Behavioral Assessment Summary

Setting Events	Immediate Triggers	Problem Behavior	Effects of Problem Behavior
	• Transition from reading to math • Independent work	• Refusal to follow directions • Pouts • Puts head down • Makes excuses	• Avoids math • Draws teacher attention

Intervention Plan

Setting Events	Immediate Triggers	Increasing Expected Behavior	Decreasing Problem Behavior

	Tier 1 Strategies
	• Active supervision
	• Behavioral momentum
	• Precorrection
		• Focus on academic success
		• Reinforcement
		  ○ Positive
		  ○ Differential reinforcement
			Tier 1 Strategies
			• Maintain the flow of instruction
			• Delayed responding

Functional Behavioral Assessment

An FBA was conducted to determine under what conditions Toby became involved in class activities and, conversely, the conditions where he would exhibit noncompliance. It became clear he was cooperative and productive in classes that involved hands-on activities, such as writing, building things, and certainly games during free time. However, when the classes did not involve using hands or movement, such as silent reading, discussions, or listening to teacher explanations, he became restless and noncooperative.

Intervention Plan

The teacher decided to select *prompting* and *opportunities to respond* as the major strategies to be used when the class is engaged in less hands-on activities, especially for discussions, silent reading, and teacher explanations. Toby would be called on more frequently for responses during discussions and explanations, and he would be prompted to keep reading and given a little more attention during silent reading. To address noncompliance, the teacher developed a *token economy* to increase cooperative behavior with Toby so that he earned points when he stayed in his seat for the three target times—silent reading, class discussions, and teacher explanations. He would receive bonus points for staying on-task during these times. A criterion was set for points earned, which gave him access to preferred hands-on activities. The teacher also arranged with him that he would need to make up any time lost, during the next break, if he decided to wander the room and not follow directions (*loss of privileges*). Toby's progress was measured by tracking the number of times he left his seat during silent reading, discussion time, and teacher explanations.

The plan depicting FBA summary and strategy selections is presented in Table 7.7, FBA Summary and Intervention Plan, Level 2 Illustration.

Level 3 Interventions: Illustration for Low-Incidence and High-Intensity Noncompliance

Initial Concern

Louisa is a capable student and usually obtains A's in her classes. However, every so often she engages in noncompliant behavior, and it escalates to more serious behavior. Basically, she tests limits by seeing how far she can go in being noncompliant. For example, when she is asked to sit down, she will slowly circle the room and stretch out the time it takes to follow the direction. If she is talking in class and is asked to quit talking and get on with her work, she will keep talking a little longer and then start her work. When she is in this mood, it doesn't matter what is asked of her—she will behave in a way that is unsatisfactory. In addition, when she is being noncompliant like this, she is looking around the class to see who is watching and does what she can to get attention from other students. The behavior ends up being quite disruptive. When she is challenged on her noncompliance and threatened with consequences, she becomes very loud and argumentative. Ultimately, she is given an office referral. Following the office referral, she settles down for a few weeks, then the cycle starts up again.

Table 7.7 FBA Summary and Intervention Plan, Level 2 Illustration (See Appendix A: FBA Summary and Intervention Plan)

Functional Behavioral Assessment Summary

Setting Events	Immediate Triggers	Problem Behavior	Effects of Problem Behavior
	Non-hands-on tasks • Discussions • Silent reading • Teacher explanations	• Intermittent compliance and noncompliance • Wanders room • Mumbling to self • Refusal to follow directions	• Avoids work • Draws teacher attention • Takes teacher time

Intervention Plan

Setting Events	Immediate Triggers	Increasing Expected Behavior	Decreasing Problem Behavior
	Tier 1 Strategies • Active supervision • Prompting • Increasing opportunities to respond • Precorrection	Tier 1 Strategies • Focus on academic success • Positive reinforcement • Token economy	Tier 1 Strategies • Maintain the flow of instruction • Loss of privileges

Functional Behavioral Assessment

Louisa's noncompliant behavior posed a challenge to her teachers because it did not occur very often, so it was difficult to conduct observations to gather the FBA information. One of the teachers decided to call a meeting with Louisa's other teachers to piece together the functional assessment information based on their collective perceptions. One teacher was assigned to interview the parents to see if there are similar cyclical issues at home and if the parents have a sense as to why she behaves in this manner at school (or at home as the case may be). Her teachers considered that she does not have close friends and that perhaps she puts on a "show" for her classmates as her way of getting their attention and approval. Louisa's mother indicated that she does not have friends stop over very much and is rarely invited to the homes of other students. All teachers were in agreement that she is a capable student and does not have problems with her academic work when she is on track. Also, the teachers indicated that they had tried the usual strategies such as precorrection, active supervision, positive reinforcement, contracts, and negative consequences, which had not been successful in changing her noncompliant behavior.

Intervention Plan

The teachers decided to target Setting Events to address her relationships with her peers (given the strategies for Immediate Triggers had been used). To this end they selected *social skills* and *parent involvement* as the strategies to be used. The school counselor ran a social-skills group twice a week, so one of the teachers and the parents encouraged her to join the group. The teachers decided to pair Louisa with other students in class as much as appropriate and to let her be a mentor to other students who needed help with their schoolwork. The parents were asked to arrange activities at home or outings in the community where Louisa could invite a friend. They also examined community sports and activities for after-school and weekend activities. A teacher and the parents decided to keep in touch weekly on how Louisa was doing in connection with other students. The other strategies the teachers decided to use were the Tier 2 Strategies for *establishing limits of behavior* and *conducting a debriefing session* to target sustained noncompliance if it occurred. It also was decided that they would use these strategies at the onset of noncompliant behavior rather than waiting until she was well into the noncompliant stance. Progress was measured by tracking the incidence of noncompliant behaviors warranting removal from the room and office referrals.

The plan depicting FBA summary and strategy selections is presented in Table 7.8, FBA Summary and Intervention Plan, Level 3 Illustration.

Level 4 Interventions: Illustration for High-Incidence and High-Intensity Noncompliance

Initial Concern

Frederick was an average student and participated in a few activities over his years in school. However, his teachers saw him as a student with a

Table 7.8 FBA Summary and Intervention Plan, Level 3 Illustration (See Appendix A: FBA Summary and Intervention Plan)

Functional Behavioral Assessment Summary

Setting Events	Immediate Triggers	Problem Behavior	Effects of Problem Behavior
• Absence of close friends at school and at home	• Class work • Student attention to her off-task behavior • Correction from teacher (in front of class) • Threat of consequences	• Refusal to follow directions • Slowly circles room • Keeps talking when asked to stop • Presses limits • Checks to see if students are watching her • Loud talk and argumentative	• Avoids work • Disrupts class • Engages class • Secures class's attention • Gains teacher time and attention • Escapes work and class

Intervention Plan

Setting Events	Immediate Triggers	Increasing Expected Behavior	Decreasing Problem Behavior

• Social skills instruction
• Parent involvement
• Afterschool sports/community activities
	Tier 1 Strategies
	• Active supervision
		• Focus on academic success
		• Reinforcement
		  ○ Positive
		  ○ Differential reinforcement
			Tier 1 Strategies
			• Maintain the flow of instruction
			
			Tier 2 Strategies
			• Establishing limits and debriefing for onset of noncompliance

very "short fuse." One teacher reported that if things didn't go his way, he would act out, disrupting the whole class. Another teacher wrote on an office referral form that he became very belligerent when he was corrected for inappropriate behavior. He has been known to threaten teachers when they followed through on his noncompliance. His school counselor reported his records showed he has had a long history of noncompliance and anger issues all the way through his schooling to his present situation in high school.

Functional Behavioral Assessment

The district behavior specialist was called in to observe Frederick and to conduct an FBA. The specialist decided to gather as much information as possible because Fredrick had such a long history with noncompliance, safety issues, and class disruption. Observations were conducted along with FBA interviews with teachers and parents. Records were also reviewed. The FBA information was quite extensive and pervasive. The major findings were (1) Frederick had problems at home and was involved with a counselor from youth services because he had threatened a neighbor on two occasions and had dumped garbage on the neighbor's front lawn; (2) he had his parents worried about his explosive behavior, especially verbal abuse, toward his younger siblings; (3) the parents reported there were times when he became very noncompliant and just would not cooperate with anything he was asked to do; (4) he exhibited low-level refusal behavior with most teachers on a frequent basis, and escalated to defiance and disrespect on occasions; (5) his relationships with peers did not appear to be a problem, and his academics were satisfactory; and (6) he was not taking medication of any kind.

Intervention Plan

The behavior specialists and teachers decided to develop an intervention plan that targeted problem behavior at school, at home, and in the community by using the *wraparound process* (Setting Events). A meeting was called involving some teachers, a specialist, parents, a youth services counselor, and an influential family member (Frederick's grandfather). At the meeting, the results of the FBA were summarized and shared. The following determinations were made for each of the parties present:

1. The behavior specialist agreed to coordinate the *wraparound process.*

2. The parents set up some chores to be done at home for which Frederick would be paid a small allowance.

3. The parents arranged a family outing involving activities for all their children on a regular basis. Low-budget options were identified.

4. The youth services counselor arranged to visit with him every other week and to involve him in the weekly anger management/conflict resolution class for youth held at the community center.

5. The teachers agreed to target the low-level noncompliant behavior by providing precorrection for the times he has more difficulty cooperating.

6. The teachers arranged for him to have a "place to go" when he became agitated to help him collect himself and avoid escalated behavior (*defusion strategies*).

7. The behavior specialist developed a *self-management* plan with Frederick to address cooperation in school and to manage his anger.

8. The teachers agreed to use the Tier 2 strategies for *limit testing* and *debriefing* when disruptive noncompliant behavior occurs.

9. All parties tracked levels of cooperation and instances of escalated behavior, especially threats.

10. The team planned to reconvene in three weeks to discuss progress and to refine the plan as needed.

11. The behavior specialist contacted each person during the three-week interval.

The plan depicting FBA summary and strategy selections is presented in Table 7.9, FBA Summary and Intervention Plan, Level 4 Illustration (see Appendix A: FBA Summary and Intervention Plan).

■ APPLICATION TO EARLIER CASE STUDIES

In Chapter 3, FBAs for Case Studies 1, 2, and 3 were presented in Tables 3.2, 3.5, and 3.7, respectively. A recap of the problem situation for each case study is presented to help the reader recall the situation. Guidelines are described for developing intervention plans for each of these case studies.

Case Study 1

> **RECAP OF BOX 3.1   NONCOMPLIANT BEHAVIOR, CASE STUDY 1**
>
> Bill often announced how much he hates math. This particular morning, just as the math period was underway, he was not following the teacher's directions. He refused to get out his notebook and was just sitting there. The teacher gave him a reminder to get started. He said he hates math, and folded his arms. The teacher pursued the refusal to cooperate with offers of assistance with the math work. Bill ended up pushing materials on the floor, muttering expletives. He was given an office referral.

A quick review of this assessment information, presented in Chapter 3, Table 3.2: FBA Summary and Intervention Plan, Case Study 1, revealed that the student had an aversion for math that probably contributed to the student's avoidance in getting started by displaying noncompliant behavior. Consequently, a major focus of a plan would be to assist the student to become more successful in math. For this determination, the teacher conducted a math assessment for the student's current level of functioning. Three possibilities may result from this assessment:

1. If the student's skills are close to the level needed for the class, the teacher would need to provide more instruction, especially in the area of additional guided practice.

Table 7.9   FBA Summary and Intervention Plan, Level 4 Illustration (See Appendix A: FBA Summary and Intervention Plan)

Functional Behavioral Assessment Summary

Setting Events	Immediate Triggers	Problem Behavior	Effects of Problem Behavior
• Long history of noncompliance • Long history of angry reactive behavior • Similar problems at home with siblings and parents • Involved with youth services	• Does not get his way • Corrections for inappropriate behavior	• Blows up in class/escalates • Makes threats • Gets angry quickly • Refuses to follow directions • Escalates when corrected • Verbal abuse • Language	• Avoids and escapes work • Disrupts class • Intimidates others • Draws attention • Creates environment of fear/concern at home and school

Intervention Plan

Setting Events	Immediate Triggers	Increasing Expected Behavior	Decreasing Problem Behavior

• Wraparound process involving school, parents, grandparent, youth services counselor
• Anger management classes
• Home plan of chores for allowance
• Visits with youth services counselor
• Self-management plan at school
	Tier 1 Strategies
	• Active supervision
	• Precorrection
		• Focus on academic success
		• Reinforcement
		  ○ Positive
		  ○ Differential reinforcement
			Tier 1 Strategies
			• Maintain the flow of instruction
			• Defusion strategies
			
			Tier 2 Strategies
			• Establishing limits and debriefing session strategy to be used for overt noncompliance

2. If the student's skill level is considerably below the level of the class, an adjustment would be made regarding the student's placement in the math program. Curriculum adaptations would be made.

3. If the student's skill level is at or above the level of the class, then there is a compliance issue that needs to be directly addressed. Incentive plans need to be introduced to encourage effort along with strategies for targeting noncompliant behavior, beginning with addressing immediate triggers.

The overall assessment result indicated that the student's skill level was just below the level required for the current content.

To design an intervention plan, strategies have been selected from the bank of strategies, Part II, Bank of Strategies for Each FBA Component. The intervention plan for this student involved strengthening his math skills to ensure success, utilizing strategies to encourage his cooperation with instruction, and encouraging his making an effort to do the work. The intervention plan, matching the initial FBA for Case Study 1, is summarized in Table 7.10, FBA Summary and Intervention Plan, Case Study 1.

Case Study 2

RECAP OF TABLE 3.4   ABC DIRECT OBSERVATION, CASE STUDY 2

The students were coming in from recess and were directed to open their reading books. One student does not follow the direction. The teacher acknowledges the class and repeats the direction to the student who still resists following the direction. The teacher gives the student a warning, and the student begins to wander around the room. The student is then given a time-out.

The FBA summary information presented for Case Study 2, in Chapter 3, Table 3.5, showed a student transitioning from recess to reading instruction in a somewhat agitated state and refusing to follow the teacher's directions to get ready for reading instruction. The situation escalated, resulting in the student being sent to the office. Based on the information observed and conversation with the teacher, the following intervention plan was developed.

1. A transition step involving the teacher reading briefly to the class following recess (as more than one student was not responding to the directions to get ready for class). This step was designed as a settling down activity following recess (defusion strategy).

2. The student's reading skills were definitely at grade level; hence, avoidance of reading was probably not an issue.

3. A precorrection plan was developed to provide reminders before recess of the need to come into class and follow directions.

4. Positive reinforcement (additional free time) would be used when the student cooperated with the initial directions for coming into class from recess.

Table 7.10 FBA Summary and Intervention Plan, Case Study 1

Functional Behavioral Assessment Summary

Setting Events	Immediate Triggers	Problem Behavior	Effects of Problem Behavior
• Aversion for math (perhaps due to history of lack of success or failure with math) • Possible lack of skills for current math class work • Issues with anger management	• The beginning of math period • Teacher directions to get materials ready • Engagement with the teacher • The warning that he would miss recess if he didn't get ready	• Refusal to follow the teacher's directions • Using bad language • Disrespect	• The teacher was drawn into the problem by student's refusal to follow directions • The student was sent to the office, thereby escaping from the math class • Class was disrupted

Intervention Plan

Setting Events	Immediate Triggers	Increasing Expected Behavior	Decreasing Problem Behavior
• Math assessment on current level of functioning • Based on results—Provide more instruction and guided practice, or • Adapt instruction and curriculum	• Active supervision • Precorrection • Behavior rehearsal	• Focus on math success • Behavioral contract • Positive reinforcement	• Delayed responding for off-task and refusal behavior • Redirection • Response cost

5. A response cost of less recess would be implemented for occasions when he did not follow directions.

6. A visit would be conducted with the recess supervisor to assess whether he was having problems with other students at recess.

This plan was then summarized in Table 7.11, Chart for FBA and Intervention Plan, Case Study 2.

Case Study 3

> ### RECAP OF TABLE 3.6   FBA INTERVIEW, CASE STUDY 3, CHAPTER 3
>
> In this FBA interview, the teacher reported the root problem was the student displayed non-compliance when asked to transition from computer time to science class. The student used many tricks to drag out her time on the computer, and it took the teacher an inordinate amount of time to get her to cooperate, all of which delays the start of science class. She is an average student, although the teacher believed she could be doing better. The resistance did not happen very frequently, but when she did resist it was very strong. The usual strategies, such as acknowledging the cooperation of other students or the threat of losing computer time on the next occasion, were not effective in securing her cooperation.

The FBA information presented for Case Study 3 was derived from a teacher interview recorded in Chapter 3, Table 3.7: FBA Summary and Intervention Plan, Case Study 3. In this instance of noncompliance, the student was refusing to transition from time on the computer to science class.

Based on this FBA information, the following steps were taken in an intervention plan to address the noncompliant behavior of the student in moving from a preferred activity to a less preferred activity.

1. Conduct a precorrection session, prior to computer time, on the need to end computer time when asked and go to the next class.

2. Use active supervision to make contact with the student during computer time.

3. Use positive reinforcement for cooperating with directions throughout the day.

4. Provide an advance prompt toward the end of computer time to remind the student to end the session punctually, and that more time will be available next time if there is good cooperation.

5. Develop a contract where the student may earn extra computer time for making a prompt transition.

6. Include a response cost component, where computer time is lessened for failure to finish on time.

7. Engage the student with other activities throughout the day to provide positive interactions (Fair-Pair rule—a common classroom practice where the student receives an equal amount of positive responses, such as praise and recognition, compared with the number of negative responses, such as corrections and reprimands).

This plan was then summarized in Table 7.12, FBA Summary and Intervention Plan, Case Study 3.

Table 7.11   Chart for FBA and Intervention Plan, Case Study 2

Functional Behavioral Assessment Summary

Setting Events	Immediate Triggers	Problem Behavior	Effects of Problem Behavior
Signs of agitation after recess, perhaps social issues at recess	Teacher direction to open reading book	Sits with arms folded, not following direction and tapping fingers	Student off task Gets teacher to repeat direction
	Teacher's personal direction and close proximity	Frowns and shuffles his feet, keeping his arms folded	Draws teacher over Gets personal direction Maintains off-task behavior
		Stands, leaves desk, and walks away from teacher	Disrupts some students Draws warning from teacher to follow directions or miss break
	Teacher raises penalty to begin reading or be sent to office	Rushes to the back of the room and is shouting	Sent to time-out area Disrupts class Escapes from reading class

Intervention Plan

Setting Events	Immediate Triggers	Increasing Expected Behavior	Decreasing Problem Behavior
Check with recess supervisor on student's social skills at recess	Defusion—Read to class immediately following recess Precorrection—Remind student of need to follow directions coming in from recess	Positive reinforcement—To reinforce following directions after recess	Response cost—Miss some recess for not following directions after recess

Table 7.12 FBA Summary and Intervention Plan, Case Study 3

Functional Behavioral Assessment Summary

Setting Events	Immediate Triggers	Problem Behavior	Effects of Problem Behavior
Grades are average Question of access to computer use and preferred activities at home	Teacher announces break time ending and gives direction to switch to science	Refuses to switch from computer to science class (transition) Ignores teacher and uses stalling tactics	Maintains time on computer
	Additional prompts from teacher, and teacher follows through with threat of losing break time next break	Becomes angry, belligerent, argumentative, and disruptive	Draws teacher over, engages teacher Delays the start of science class
	Told she is losing her next break	Still takes her time and eventually wanders over to science class	Gets out of science with escalation Misses next break time Makes everyone wait Continues with computer Misses next computer time

Intervention Plan

Setting Events	Immediate Triggers	Increasing Expected Behavior	Decreasing Problem Behavior
Check with parents on availability of computer at home Relationship building—Structure opportunities for student to help during day (Fair-Pair rule)	Precorrection to explain expectations for computer time Active supervision—Make contact during computer time Provide advance prompt toward end of computer time	Positive reinforcement for cooperation during the day Contract using extra computer time for quick transition	Use response cost—Less computer time for lack of cooperation when student does not finish with computer on time

CHAPTER SUMMARY ■

The overall approach for addressing noncompliant behavior in the classroom is to conduct an FBA and to use this information to develop an intervention plan. The process is typically initiated by a teacher who notices that a student is beginning to show noncompliant behavior, or the student has been displaying noncompliant behavior for some time, and the strategies commonly used in the classroom are not working.

Many research-based practices in published literature exist for managing problem behavior, including noncompliant behavior, which at first glance, can be quite overwhelming. Educators need to have a plan of attack for determining which strategies to use or which combination of strategies to select. A major guideline for these determinations can be derived from an accurate FBA. The FBA and data system provide information on the intensity and frequency of the problem behavior, which determines the time, effort, and cost in developing and implementing an effective intervention plan. In this chapter, four levels of intervention were generated by considering the interaction between high and low frequency and high and low intensity of the noncompliant behavior. Corresponding intervention plans were then presented for each of these levels. Finally, case studies arising from FBA information presented in Chapter 3 were completed by generating intervention plans of each case.

8

The Road Map

There are many details in conducting a functional behavioral assessment (FBA) and in selecting appropriate strategies in developing an intervention plan. The purpose of this final chapter is to provide direction to the reader by describing a road map linking the FBA with a bank of strategies. The road map consists of an FBA summary in which the key questions are listed for the FBA (Chapter 3) followed by a corresponding list of strategies for each of the FBA components drawn from Chapters 4, 5, and 6 (see Table 8.1, Master Chart for FBA Summary and Intervention Plan: The Road Map [see also the insert at the end of this book]).

To assist the reader in recalling the various strategies listed in the master chart, a glossary of terms is presented in Box 8.1, Glossary of Terms for FBA Strategies, which is also included in the insert at the end of the book. The chapter ends with concluding remarks.

BOX 8.1 GLOSSARY OF TERMS FOR FBA STRATEGIES (SEE INSERT AT THE END OF THE BOOK)

Immediate Triggers

Tier 1 Strategies require the least time, effort, or cost.

  Active Supervision is a type of monitoring procedure involving moving around, scanning all areas, and interacting with the students at a reasonably high rate.

  Behavioral Momentum is a teaching technique using high-probability tasks to achieve a subsequent low-probability task by presenting a series of easy or enjoyable requests quickly followed with a more difficult request.

Defusing Techniques are empathetic strategies designed to assist agitated students to calm down and resume the class activity.

Pacing is an instructional technique used by teachers to maintain the flow of instruction by ensuring that the *rate* of instructional delivery is sufficiently high to engage the students and keep them on task.

Prompting involves providing additional information, such as a hint, cue, or gesture, just prior to engaging the student in a task so that there is more likelihood of acceptable behavior occurring versus problem behavior.

Opportunities to Respond is an instructional strategy designed to provide *all* students with sufficient opportunities to be actively engaged in the lesson.

Tier 2 Strategies typically take more time, effort, or cost.

Behavior Rehearsal involves creating successive approximations of the context likely to trigger noncompliance and providing the student with *practice* in making the expected response versus the predictable problem behavior.

Context Modification is designed to slightly change the setting where the noncompliant behavior occurs so that the student is more likely to exhibit the expected behavior and less likely to be noncompliant.

Fading is a technique for systematically phasing out levels of support provided by the intervention used to address noncompliance to the normal supports used in the classroom.

Minimizing Errors involves accurate assessment of the student's skill level and very carefully sequencing content so that the student is highly likely to produce correct responses.

Precorrection is based on knowing the triggers that set off the problem behavior and intervening *before* the triggers can operate, thereby preempting the problem behavior.

Task Interspersal is a strategy designed to increase on-task behavior by presenting a planned mix of easy tasks with more difficult tasks to the students.

Setting Events

Academic Assessment and Instructional Decision Making is a critical strategy if the noncompliant behavior occurs during or just before instruction. This strategy involves ensuring that the student's skill level is adequate for the task, and, if not, adjustments are made to instruction for this student.

Anger Management programs are designed for students who display high rates of anger. These programs, formal and informal, are intended to *teach* students skills for identifying what makes them angry, followed by strategies for dealing with their anger.

Conflict Resolution programs, formal and informal, provide students with skills to solve problems peacefully and constructively.

(Continued)

(Continued)

Curriculum Intervention is needed when academic assessment shows the student's skill level is not at the level required by the curriculum or shows that the curriculum is poorly designed and several students in the class are having problems.

Instructional Delivery refers to the methods used to teach the lesson content. The bottom line is that the method needs to engage the class in productive and accurate responses.

Individual Behavior Instruction Plan is a formal technique for *teaching* an individual student how to behave appropriately. The same teaching strategies are used to teach behavior as are used to teach other skills.

Parent Involvement is the ideal situation for helping a student learn new behaviors to be exhibited both at school and at home. These partnerships are formed between school personnel and parents with ongoing communication and training as appropriate.

Teacher-Student Relationship is often a necessary condition for some students to be reached in order to change their behavior. Teachers are encouraged to do what they can to establish and maintain a productive and trustworthy relationship with students who need extra help.

Self-Management Skills is an approach where students learn to take charge of their own behavior with a systematic plan developed and monitored with teacher support.

Social Skills Instruction makes use of formal and informal programs designed to *teach* students social skills. The target students typically display antisocial behavior and need to be directly taught prosocial behavior.

Wraparound Process is an approach particularly appropriate for students who are exhibiting problem behaviors at school, home, and in the community. Key players from all involved agencies, parents, and school personnel work closely together in developing and implementing a systematic, integrated plan to ensure the student becomes successful in all settings.

Effects of Problem Behavior

Increasing Expected Behavior

Focus on Academic Success is a fundamental priority practice for teachers whether students have problem behavior or not. This strategy helps teachers constantly watch for student progress and make instructional adjustments as needed to ensure academic success.

Behavioral Contracts are incentive plans for increasing student desirable behavior and decreasing problem behavior. The plan involves student access to privileges or rewards for meeting criteria in the plan, and student buy-in is the key for success.

Reinforcement is defined in terms of its function. Something can be said to be reinforcing if it results in increasing certain behaviors.

- **Positive Reinforcement** is the contingent delivery of something that is perceived to be desirable for the student, used to increase occurrences of a target behavior.
- **Negative Reinforcement** is the contingent removal of something that is perceived to be undesirable by the student, used to increase occurrences of a target behavior.

- **Differential Reinforcement** refers to the delivery of reinforcement contingent on the occurrence of appropriate behavior and withholding of reinforcement in the presence of inappropriate behavior under the same or similar conditions.

Shaping is the process of successively reinforcing closer approximations of the target behavior to the criterion or acceptable level of behavior.

Token Economies involve setting up a plan with a student where the student earns tokens for exhibiting a target behavior and may exchange the tokens for reinforcers to be used at another time.

Reducing Problem Behavior

Tier 1 Strategies require the least amount of attention and interruption to instruction and are used by teachers to reduce occurrences of the problem behavior.

Maintain the Flow of Instruction is the very first response of the teacher when noncompliance is exhibited. The teacher makes a concerted effort to delay responding to the problem behavior by continuing with the lesson or activity (unless, of course, safety issues or severe disruption are involved).

Delayed Responding, sometimes called planned ignoring, involves the teacher noticing the noncompliant behavior of the student and making a conscious decision to continue with instruction as if nothing had happened, directly acknowledging students who are cooperating. However, if the student persists with noncompliance, then more direct steps would be taken.

Extinction is the generic term used to describe the process for the discontinuation or withholding of the reinforcers that are maintaining a target behavior.

Redirection Prompts or cues are designed to assist the student to focus on the request provided by the teacher, or expected behavior, with *minimum attention* given to the student.

Rule Restatement is a strategy where the teacher directly secures the student's attention and restates the rule or expectation so there is no misunderstanding of what is required of the student.

Tier 2 Strategies are designed as a *bottom line* or *last resort* type of classroom intervention to be implemented when the Tier 1 and other proactive strategies have been unsuccessful in changing the target problem behavior.

Part A: Establishing Limits of Behavior in which clear communication is provided to the student that cooperation is expected, or there will be negative consequence. The steps are to (1) set up the procedures beforehand with the students; (2) present the expected behavior and the negative consequence as a decision for the student to make; (3) allow a few seconds for the student to make the decision; (4) withdraw and attend to the other students; and (5) follow through based on the student's decision.

Part B: Conducting a Debriefing Session is a problem-solving strategy following a noncompliant incident for equipping the student to handle similar situations better in the future. Typically, the student is assisted to address three questions: "What did I do?" "Why did I do it?" and "What else could I have done?"

Table 8.1 Master Chart for FBA Summary and Intervention Plan: The Road Map (See Insert at the End of the Book)

Functional Behavioral Assessment Summary			
Setting Events	*Immediate Triggers*	*Problem Behavior*	*Effects of Problem Behavior*
Has the student experienced setbacks with demand before, such as: • Failure • Embarrassment or ridicule • Rejection • Injury • Punishment • Other What basis is there to know if the student can perform the task satisfactorily? Have there been previous attempts to address the noncompliance? Are there nonclassroom-based risk factors, such as: • Home issues • Hunger • Substance abuse • Inadequate sleep • Transportation to school problems • Peer conflicts • Other	What is the task or demand required? What words are used by staff in presenting the demand? What are the prerequisite skills for the task? Does the involved student have the prerequisite skills to complete the task? Has the student been on task prior to this demand situation? Other?	What does the student do to noncomply? What language does the student use when noncomplying? How does the student avoid the demand or task? How does the student escape the demand or task? How does the student not fulfill the task to a reasonable standard? What do the other students do in this context that is acceptable? Other?	What changes occur in the setting when the noncompliance occurs? What does the teacher do immediately following the noncompliance? What does the teacher say following noncompliance? What consequences are delivered? What do other students do/say when the noncompliance occurs? Are other adults brought into the picture? Does instruction or the activity stop? Other?

Intervention Plan

Setting Events	Immediate Triggers	Problem Behavior	Effects of Problem Behavior

- Academic assessment and instructional decision making
- Anger management
- Conflict resolution
- Curriculum intervention
- Instructional delivery
- Individual behavior instruction plan
- Parent involvement
- Self-management skills
- Social skills instruction
- Teacher-student relationship
- Wraparound process
- Other
	Tier 1 Strategies
	
	- Active supervision
	- Behavioral momentum
	- Defusing techniques
	- Pacing
	- Prompting
	- Opportunities to respond
	- Other
	
	Tier 2 Strategies
	
	- Behavior rehearsal
	- Context modification
	- Fading
	- Minimizing errors
	- Precorrection
	- Task interspersal
	- Stimulus control
	- Other
		- Focus on academic success
		- Behavioral contracts
		- Reinforcement
		  - Positive
		  - Negative
		  - Differential reinforcement
		- Shaping
		- Token economies
		- Other
			Tier 1 Strategies
			
			- Maintain the flow of instruction
			- Delayed responding
			- Extinction
			- Redirection prompts
			- Rule restatement
			- Other
			
			Tier 2 Strategies
			
			- Part A: Establishing limits of behavior
			- Part B: Conducting a debriefing session
			- Other

■ CONCLUDING REMARKS

Classroom teachers often face significant challenges with problem behavior in general, and noncompliant behavior in particular. It has been well established in research that noncompliant behavior is one of the most frequently occurring problem behaviors teachers struggle with on a regular basis from kindergarten through high school. Moreover, one of the most common expectations teachers have of their students is to follow directions and cooperate in class.

It is argued in this book that noncompliance cannot be effectively addressed through a one-dimensional strategy, or what is commonly referred to as a "silver bullet" approach. The mere fact that this behavior ranks as the most common reason for office referrals, K–12, is testimony that a simple approach to the problem is not effective. Rather, many factors contribute to noncompliant behavior, or any problem behavior for that matter, which means that a systemic approach is needed to effectively address this problem behavior.

First and foremost, schools and districts must make success in school, especially academic achievement, an attainable goal for all students. There is a growing data base showing where schools and districts have developed and implemented systematic school improvement plans resulting in significant gains in academic achievement. Ample evidence also exists to support the claim that if all students are productively engaged in instruction and experience academic success, there will be substantially less behavior problems in the classroom. Consequently, if schools have a highly focused and visible agenda to improve student achievement, classroom teachers will be in a much stronger position to expect cooperation and to address noncompliant behavior.

A second systemic approach for addressing problem behavior in classrooms is for schools and districts to adopt and maintain a proactive schoolwide behavioral support plan. These schoolwide efforts target cooperative behavior on a schoolwide basis, which of course includes classrooms, and provide structures for students who may need more direct support to effectively change their behavior. Once these two systemic approaches for academic improvement and schoolwide behavior are firmly in place, teachers and specialist are in strategic positions to address noncompliant behavior and other problems in their classroom (Colvin, 2007).

A major reason why noncompliant behavior has assumed such prevalence and concern among educators is that it may not be properly understood. For this reason, efforts were made in this book to carefully define noncompliant behavior to capture the many nuances of this behavior.

Another area targeted in this book is the issue of behavioral assessment. It is argued that an accurate assessment of behavior enables the teacher and specialist to generate explanations for the behavior and develop precise intervention plans. To this end, procedures for conducting and using FBAs of noncompliance are described in detail.

It is presumed that if a teacher has solid information on noncompliant behavior, arising from a reliable FBA, it is relatively straightforward to generate an effective intervention plan. However, there exists in the literature, and best practices in general, a deep array of evidence-based strategies for addressing problem behavior. Many of these strategies have been described and illustrated with guidelines for determining which strategies to select in developing specific intervention plans.

An overall road map reflecting the interface between an FBA and resulting intervention plan and a glossary of terms is presented in an insert. This chart depicts key questions to be considered for each component of an FBA, a bank of corresponding strategies that could be selected in developing an intervention plan, and a glossary of terms for the strategies.

It is hoped that teachers, specialists, and behavior support team members realize that noncompliant behavior can be effectively addressed. The combination of the vigorous pursuit of systemic factors, academic achievement, and schoolwide behavior support, along with systematic use of FBAs, intervention plans, and the road map, will enable educators to be successful in managing problem behavior and achieving their educational goals for all students.

Appendices

Note: These appendices may be reproduced or adapted for personal use in the classroom, school, or district.

Appendix A FBA Summary and Intervention Plan

Functional Behavioral Assessment (FBA) Summary

Setting Events	Immediate Triggers	Problem Behavior	Effects of Problem Behavior

Intervention Plan

Setting Events	Immediate Triggers	Increasing Expected Behavior	Decreasing Problem Behavior

Appendix B FBA Checklist for Noncompliance

Functional Behavioral Assessment (FBA) Summary

Setting Events	Immediate Triggers	Problem Behavior	Effects of Problem Behavior
Has the student experienced setbacks with demand before, such as: • Failure • Embarrassment or ridicule • Rejection • Injury • Punishment • Other What basis is there to know if the student can perform the task satisfactorily? Have there been previous attempts to address the noncompliance? Are there nonclassroom-based risk factors such as: • Home issues • Hunger • Substance abuse • Inadequate sleep • Transportation to school problems • Peer conflicts • Other	What is the task or demand required? What words are used by staff in presenting the demand? What are the prerequisite skills for the task? Does the involved student have the prerequisite skills to complete the task? Has the student been on task prior to this demand situation? Other?	What does the student do to non-comply? What language does the student use when noncomplying? How does the student avoid the demand or task? How does the student escape the demand or task? How does the student not fulfill the task to a reasonable standard? What do the other students do in this context that is acceptable? Other?	What changes occur in the setting when the noncompliance occurs? What does the teacher do immediately following the noncompliance? What does the teacher say following noncompliance? What consequences are delivered? What do other students do/say when the noncompliance occurs? Are other adults brought into the picture? Does instruction or the activity stop? Other?

Intervention Plan

Setting Events	Immediate Triggers	Increasing Expected Behavior	Decreasing Problem Behavior

Appendix C ABC Direct Observation Form

Student Name: _____ Observation Date: _____

Observer: _____ Begin Time: _____ End Time: _____

Activity: _____ Class Period: _____

Notes (Potential Setting Events)	Antecedents (Immediate Triggers)	Behavior (Problem Behavior)	Consequences (Effects of Problem Behavior)

Appendix D FBA Interview Form

Teacher's Name: _____

Date: _____

Interviewer: _____

Begin Time: _____   End Time: _____

Student's Name: _____

Grade Level: _____

FBA Information

Problem Behavior: Noncompliance

What does the student do to noncomply?

What language does the student use when noncomplying?

How does the student avoid the demand or task?

How does the student escape the demand or task?

How does the student not fulfill the task to a reasonable standard?

What do the other students do in this context that is acceptable?

Other?

Immediate Triggers

What is the specific task that is required of the students when the noncompliance occurs?

What words are used by staff in presenting the demand?

What are the prerequisite skills for the task?

Does the involved student have the prerequisite skills to complete the task?

Has the student been on-task prior to this demand situation?

Other?

Setting Events
 	
Has the student experienced anything aversive with this demand situation before, such as:
 	
   • Failure
   • Embarrassment or ridicule
   • Rejection
   • Injury
   • Punishment
   • Other
 	
Is there a basis to know that the student can perform the task correctly?
 	
Have there been previous attempts to address the noncompliance?
 	
Are there nonclassroom based factors that put the student in a negative frame of mind, such as:
 	
   • Home issues
   • Hunger
   • Substance abuse
   • Inadequate sleep
   • Transportation to school problems
   • Peer conflicts
   • Other
 	
Other?	

Effects of the Problem Behavior What changes occur in the setting where the noncompliance is occurring? What does the teacher do immediately following the noncompliance? What does the teacher say following noncompliance? What consequences are delivered? What do other students do/say when the noncompliance occurs? Are other adults brought into the picture? Does instruction or the activity stop? Other?	

(Continued)

(Continued)

Additional Information	
Data What classroom data do you have on the student's noncompliance? Are there office referral data? What are the student's grades?	
Strategies Used What have you tried to address the problem? What strategies have had some success? What strategies may have escalated the student's behavior?	
Strengths and Reinforcers What subjects are strengths? What activities engage the student? What are the reinforcers for the student?	

Appendix E   Record Review Checklist

Student Name: Reviewer's Name:	Grade: Review Date:

Office Referrals

Noncompliance

☐ Frequency
☐ Location
☐ Faculty
☐ Subject
☐ Period of time
☐ History
☐ Other

Other Office Referrals

☐ Skipping class
☐ Fighting
☐ Bullying, harassment, hazing
☐ Other

School Performance

☐ Grades
☐ Participation in school events
☐ Attendance
☐ Peer group relationships
☐ Faculty relationships
☐ Other

Risk Factors

☐ Possession of illegal weapons
☐ Vandalism at school, home, community
☐ Transiency
☐ Gang activity
☐ Truancy
☐ School suspensions or expulsions
☐ Court adjudicated
☐ Parents withdrawing student from school
☐ Child abuse
☐ Poverty
☐ Other

Appendix F Bank of Strategies for Each FBA Component

Functional Behavioral Assessment Summary

Setting Events	Immediate Triggers	Problem Behavior	Effects of Problem Behavior

Intervention Plan

Setting Events	Immediate Triggers	Increasing Expected Behavior	Decreasing Problem Behavior

• Academic assessment and instructional decision making
• Anger management
• Conflict resolution
• Curriculum intervention
• Instructional delivery
• Individual behavior instruction plan
• Parent involvement
• Teacher-student relationship
• Self-management skills
• Social skills instruction
• Wraparound process
• Other
	Tier 1 Strategies
	• Active supervision
	• Behavioral momentum
	• Defusing techniques
	• Pacing
	• Prompting
	• Opportunities to respond
	• Other
	
	Tier 2 Strategies
	• Behavior rehearsal
	• Context modification
	• Fading
	• Minimizing errors
	• Precorrection
	• Task interspersal
	• Stimulus control
	• Other
		• Focus on academic success
		• Behavioral contracts
		• Reinforcement
		  ○ Positive
		  ○ Negative
		  ○ Differential reinforcement
		• Shaping
		• Token economies
		• Other
			Tier 1 Strategies
			• Maintain the flow of instruction
			• Delayed responding
			• Extinction
			• Redirection prompts
			• Rule restatement
			• Other
			
			Tier 2 Strategies
			• Part A: Establishing limits of behavior
			• Part B: Conducting a debriefing session
			• Other

References

Alberto, P. A., & Troutman, A. C. (2003). *Applied behavior analysis for teachers* (6th ed.). Upper Saddle River, NJ: Merrill/Prentice Hall.

Albin, R. (2005). Fading. In M. Hersen, G. Sugai, & R. Horner (Eds.), *Encyclopedia of behavior modification and cognitive behavior therapy: Vol. 3* (pp. 1315–1317). Thousand Oaks, CA: Sage Publications.

Algozzine, R., & Konrad, M. (2005). Direct observation. In M. Herson, G. Sugai, & R. Horner (Eds.), *Encyclopedia of behavior modification and cognitive behavior therapy: Vol. 3.* (pp. 1266–1269). Thousand Oaks, CA: Sage Publications.

Auerbach, S., & Smith, V. (2005). Negative reinforcement. In M. Hersen, G. Sugai, & R. Horner (Eds.), *Encyclopedia of behavior modification and cognitive behavior therapy: Vol. 3* (pp.1395–1398). Thousand Oaks, CA: Sage Publications.

Ayllon, T. (1999). *How to use token economy and point systems* (2nd ed.). Austin, TX: Pro-Ed.

Belfiore, P. J., Pulley Basile, S., & Lee, D. L. (2008). Using a high probability command sequence to increase classroom compliance: The role of behavioral momentum. *Journal of Behavioral Education, 17*(2), 160–171.

Bernal, M. E., Klinnert, M. D., & Schultz, L. A. (1980). Outcome evaluation of behavioral parent training and client-centered parent counseling for children with conduct problems. *Journal of Applied Behavior Analysis, 13,* 677–691.

Burke, M., & Crowder, C. (2005). Differential reinforcement. In M. Hersen, G. Sugai, & R. Horner (Eds.), *Encyclopedia of behavior modification and cognitive behavior therapy: Vol. 3* (pp. 1132–1135). Thousand Oaks, CA: Sage Publications.

Burns, B. J., & Goldman, S. K. (1999). *Promising practices in wraparound for children with serious emotional disturbance and their families: Systems of care.* Washington, DC: Center for Effective Collaboration and Practice, American Institute for Research.

Carr, J., & Wilder, D. A. (2004). *Functional assessment and intervention: A guide to understanding behavior* (2nd ed.). Homewood, IL: High Tide Press.

Carr, S. C., & Punzo, R. P. (1993). The effects of self-monitoring on academic accuracy and productivity on the performance of students with behavioral disorders. *Behavioral Disorders, 18*(4), 241–250.

Carr, T. (2005). *141 creative strategies for reaching adolescents with anger problems.* Chapin, NC: Youthlight, Inc.

Cartledge, G. (2005). Behavioral rehearsal. In M. Hersen, G. Sugai, & R. Horner (Eds.), *Encyclopedia of behavior modification and cognitive behavior therapy: Vol. 3* (pp. 1198–1200). Thousand Oaks, CA: Sage Publications.

Cates, G. L. (2005). A review of the effects of interspersing procedures on the stages of academic skill development. *Journal of Behavioral Education, 14*(4), 303–325.

Chandler, L. K., & Dahlquist, C. M. (2005). *Functional assessment: Strategies to prevent and remediate challenging behavior in school settings.* Upper Saddle River, NJ: Prentice-Hall/Pearson Education.

Cipani, E., & Schock, K. (2007). *Functional behavioral assessment, diagnosis, and treatment: A complete system for education and mental health settings.* New York: Springer Publishing Company.

Cohen, R. (1995). *Students resolving conflict: Peer mediation in schools.* Tucson, AZ: Good Year Books.

Colvin, G. (1999). *Defusing anger and aggression: Safe strategies for secondary school educators* [Video/DVD program]. Eugene, OR: Iris Media.

Colvin, G. (2004). *Managing the cycle of acting-out behavior in the classroom.* Eugene, OR: Behavior Associates.

Colvin, G. (2005a). *Managing non-compliance: Effective strategies for K–12 teachers* [Video/DVD program]. Eugene, OR: Iris Media.

Colvin, G. (2005b). Precorrection: Anticipating problem behavior. In M. Hersen, G. Sugai, & R. Horner (Eds.), *Encyclopedia of behavior modification and cognitive behavior therapy: Vol. 3* (pp. 1437–1441). Thousand Oaks, CA: Sage Publications.

Colvin, G. (2007). *7 steps for developing a proactive schoolwide discipline plan: A guide for principals and leadership teams.* Thousand Oaks, CA: Corwin.

Colvin, G., Kame'enui, E., & Sugai, G. (1993). Reconceptualizing behavior management and school-wide discipline in general education. *Education and Treatment of Children, 16*(4), 361–381.

Colvin, G., & Lazar, M. (1997). *The effective elementary classroom: Managing for success.* Longmont, CO: Sopris West Educational Services.

Colvin, G., Sugai, G., Good, R. H., & Lee, Y. (1997). Using active supervision and precorrection to improve transition behaviors in an elementary school. *School Psychology Quarterly, 12*(4), 344–363.

Cotton, K. (2000). *The schooling practices that matter most.* Alexandria, VA: Association for Supervision and Curriculum Development.

Cummings, C. (2000). *Winning strategies for classroom management.* Alexandria, VA: Association for Supervision and Curriculum Development.

Darch, C. B., & Kame'enui, E. J. (2004). *Instructional classroom management: A proactive approach to classroom management* (2nd ed.). Upper Saddle River, NJ: Pearson Education.

Diffily, D., & Sassman, C. (2006). *Positive teacher talk for better classroom management, grades K-2.* New York: Scholastic.

Dishion, T. J., French, D. C., & Patterson, G. R. (1995). The development and ecology of antisocial behavior. In D. Cicchetti & D. J. Cohen (Eds.), *Developmental psychopathology: Vol. 2. Risk, disorder, and adaptation* (pp. 421–471). New York: John Wiley & Sons.

Dowd, T., & Tierney, J. (2005). *Teaching social skills to youth* (2nd ed.). Boys Town, NE: Boys Town Press.

Eber, L. (2003). *The art and science of wraparound: Completing the continuum of school-wide behavioral support.* Bloomington, IN: Forum on Education at Indiana University.

Eber, L., Hyde, K., Rose, J., Breen, K., McDonald, D., & Lewandowski, H. (in press). Completing the continuum of school-wide positive behavior support: Wraparound as a tertiary level intervention. In W. Sailor, G. Dunlap, G. Sugai, & R. Horner (Eds.), *Handbook of positive behavior support.* New York: Springer.

Eddy, J. M. (2001). *Aggressive and defiant behavior: The latest assessment and treatment strategies for the conduct disorders* (2nd ed.). Kansas City, MO: Compact Clinicals.

Engelmann, S. (1993). The curriculum as the cause of failure. In J. Marr, G. Sugai, & G. Tindal (Eds.), *The Oregon conference monograph 1993* (pp. 3–8). Eugene: University of Oregon, College of Education.

Engelmann, S., & Carnine, D. (1991). *Theory of instruction.* Eugene, OR: Association for Direct Instruction Press.

Engelmann, S., & Colvin, G. (2007). *Rubric for identifying authentic direct instruction programs*. Eugene, OR: Engelmann Foundation.

Epstein, J. L., Sanders, M. G., Simon, B. S., Clark Salinas, N., Rodriguez Jansorn, N., & Van Voorhis, F. L. (2002). *School, family, and community partnerships: Your handbook for action*. Thousand Oaks, CA: Corwin.

Forgatch, M. S., & Patterson, G. R. (2005). *Parents and adolescents living together: Part 2. Family problem solving* (2nd ed.). Champaign, IL: Research Press.

Frase, L., & Hetzel, R. (1990). *School management by wandering around*. Lancaster, PA: Technomic Publishing Company.

Fuchs, D., & Deshler, D. D. (2007). What we need to know about responsiveness to intervention (and shouldn't be afraid to ask). *Learning Disabilities Research & Practice, 22*, 129–136.

Girard, K., & Koch, S. J. (1996). *Conflict resolution in the schools: A manual for educators*. San Francisco: Jossey-Bass Publishers.

Gunter, P. L., & Conroy, M. A. (1998). Increasing correct academic responding: An effective intervention strategy to decrease behavior problems. *Effective School Practices, 17*(2), 55–62.

Hale, J. B. (2006). Implementing IDEA with a three-tier model that includes response to intervention and cognitive assessment methods. *School Psychology Forum: Research and Practice, 1*, 16–27.

Hawken, L. S., & Burrow-Sanchez, J. J. (2005). *Behavioral contracting*. In M. Hersen, G. Sugai, & R. Horner (Eds.), *Encyclopedia of behavior modification and cognitive behavior therapy: Vol. 3* (pp. 1180–1182). Thousand Oaks, CA: Sage Publications.

Hieneman, M., Nolan, M., Presley, J., De Turo, L., Roberson, W., & Dunlap, G. (1999). *Facilitator's guide: Positive behavioral support*. Tallahassee, FL: Positive Behavioral Support Project, Florida Department of Education.

Hunter, R. (2004). *Madeline Hunter's mastery teaching*. Thousand Oaks, CA: Corwin.

Jones, V. F., & Jones, J. (2006). *Comprehensive classroom management: Creating communities of support and problem solving*. Boston: Allyn & Bacon.

Kalb, L. M., & Loeber, R. (2003). Child disobedience and noncompliance: A review. *Pediatrics, 3*(3), 641–652.

Kauffman, J. M. (1997). *Characteristics of emotionally and behavioral disorders of children and youth* (6th ed.). Columbus, OH: Merrill.

Kern, L., & Clemens, N. H. (2005). Task interspersal. In M. Hersen, G. Sugai, & R. Horner (Eds.), *Encyclopedia of behavior modification and cognitive behavior therapy: Vol. 3* (pp. 1565–1568). Thousand Oaks, CA: Sage Publications.

Kern, L., & Starosta, K. M. (2004). Behavioral momentum. In M. Hersen, G. Sugai, & R. Horner (Eds.), *Encyclopedia of behavior modification and cognitive behavior therapy: Vol. 3* (pp. 1189–1190). Thousand Oaks, CA: Sage Publications.

Knoff, H. M. (2001). *Stop and think social skills program*. Longmont, CO: Sopris West Educational Services.

Kochanska, G., Aksan, N., & Koenig, A. L. (1995). A longitudinal study of the roots of preschoolers' conscience: Committed compliance and emerging internalization. *Child Development, 66*, 1752–1769.

Lane, K. L. (2005). Extinction. In M. Hersen, G. Sugai, & R. Horner (Eds.), *Encyclopedia of behavior modification and cognitive behavior therapy: Vol. 3* (pp. 1311–1314). Thousand Oaks, CA: Sage Publications.

Lane, K. L., Wehby, J. H., & Cooley, C. (2006). Teacher expectations of students' classroom behavior across the grade span: Which social skills are necessary for success? *Exceptional Children, 72*(2), 153–167.

Luiselli, J. K. (2005). Stimulus control. In M. Hersen, G. Sugai, & R. Horner (Eds.), *Encyclopedia of behavior modification and cognitive behavior therapy: Vol. 3* (pp. 1548–1552). Thousand Oaks, CA: Sage Publications.

Maag, J. W. (2004). *Behavior management: From theoretical implications to practical applications* (2nd ed.). Belmont, CA: Wadsworth/Thompson Learning.

Marion, M. (1997). Guiding young children's understanding and management of anger. *Young Children, 52*(7), 62–67.

May, S., Ard, W., Todd, A. W., Horner, R. H., Glasgow, A., Sugai, G., & Sprague, J. (2003). *School-wide information system*. Eugene: Educational and Community Supports, University of Oregon.

Mayer, R. G. (1998). Constructive discipline for school personnel. *Education and Treatment of Children, 22,* 36–54.

McGinnis, E., & Goldstein, A. P. (2003). *Skillstreaming in early childhood: New strategies for teaching prosocial social skills* (Rev. ed.). Champaign, IL: Research Press.

Nelson, J. R., Roberts, M. L., & Smith, D. (1998). *Conducting functional behavioral assessment: A practical guide*. Longmont, CO: Sopris West Educational Services.

Newcomer, L., & Lewis, T. J. (2005). Active supervision. M. Hersen, G. Sugai, & R. Horner (Eds.), *Encyclopedia of behavior modification and cognitive behavior therapy: Vol. 3* (pp. 1132–1135). Thousand Oaks, CA: Sage Publications.

O'Neill, R. E., Horner, R. H., Albin, R. W., Storey, K., Sprague, J., & Newton, J. S. (1997). *Functional assessment and program development for problem behavior: A practical handbook* (2nd ed.). Pacific Grove, CA: Brooks/Cole.

Patterson, G. R., & Forgatch, M. S. (2005). *Parents and adolescents living together: Part 1: The basics* (2nd ed.). Champaign, IL: Research Press.

Patterson, G. R., Ray, R. S., Shaw, D. A., & Cobb, J. A. (1969). *Manual for coding of family interactions*. Eugene, OR: Castalia.

Print, M. (1993). *Curriculum development and design*. Sydney, Australia: Allen & Unwin Book Publishers.

Rhode, G., Jensen, W., & Reavis, H. K. (1992). *The tough kid book: Practical classroom management strategies*. Longmont, CO: Sopris West Educational Services.

Shapiro, E. S. (1994). *Behavior change in the classroom: Self-management interventions*. New York: Guilford Press.

Shapiro, E. S. (2004). *Academic skills: Direct assessment and intervention*. New York: Guilford Press.

Shores, R. E., Gunter, P. L., & Jack, S. L. (1993). Classroom management strategies: Are they setting events for coercion? *Behavioral Disorders, 18*(2), 92–102.

Skiba, R. J., Peterson, R. L., & Williams, T. (1997). Office referrals and suspension: disciplinary intervention in middle schools. *Education and Treatment of Children, 20,* 295–315.

Spaulding, S. A., Horner, R. H., Irvin L. K., May, S. L., Emeldi, M., Tobin, T. J., & Sugai, G. (2008). School-wide social-behavioral climate, student problem behavior, support needs, and related administrative decision-making: Empirical patterns from 2005–06 database on 1709 schools nationwide. Manuscript under review.

Sprague, J. R. & Golly, A. (2004). *Best behavior: Building positive behavior support in schools*. Longmont, CO: Sopris West Educational Services.

Sprick, R., & Garrison, M. (2008). *Interventions: Evidence-based behavioral strategies for individual students* (2nd ed.). Eugene, OR: Pacific Northwest Publishing.

Sprick, R., Garrison, M., & Howard, L. (1998). *CHAMPs: A proactive and positive approach to classroom management*. Longmont, CO: Sopris West Educational Services.

Sprick, R., Wise, B., Marcum, K., Haykim, M., & Howard, L. (2005). *Administrator's desk reference of behavioral management (Vols. I, II, III)*. Eugene, OR: Pacific Northwest Publishing.

Starkman, N. (2006). *Connecting in your classroom: 18 teachers tell how they foster the relationships that lead to student success*. Minneapolis, MN: Search Institute.

Stewart, J. (2002). *The anger workbook for teens*. Torrance, CA: Jalmar Press.

Stiggins, R. J. (2001). *Student-involved student assessment* (3rd ed.). Columbus, OH: Merrill Prentice Hall.

Sugai, G., & Colvin, G. (1997). Debriefing: A transition step for promoting acceptable behavior. *Education and Treatment of Children, 20,* 209–221.

Sugai, G., & Horner, R. H. (2005). School-wide positive behavior supports: Achieving and sustaining effective learning environments for all students. In W. H. Heward (Ed.), *Focus on behavior analysis in education: Achievements, challenges, and opportunities* (pp. 90–102). Upper Saddle River, NJ: Pearson Prentice-Hall.

Sugai, G., Horner, R. H., & Gresham, F. M. (2002). Behaviorally effective school environments. In M. Shinn, H. M. Walker, & M. Stoner (Eds.), *Interventions for academic and behavior problems II: Preventive and remedial approaches* (pp. 315–350). Bethesda, MD: NASP Publications.

Sugai, G., & Tindal, G. A. (1995). *Effective school consultation: An interactive approach.* Pacific Grove, CA: Brooks/Cole.

Sutherland, K. S. (2003). The effect of varying rates of opportunities to respond to academic requests on the classroom behavior of students with EBD. *Journal of Emotional and Behavioral Disorders, 11*(4), 239–248.

Sutherland, K. S., Wehby, J. H., & Yoder, P. J. (2002). Examination of the relationship between teacher praise and opportunity for students with EBD to respond to academic requests and the academic and behavioral outcomes of students with EBD: A review. *Journal of Emotional & Behavioral Disorders, 22*(2), 113–121.

Tindal, G., & Haladyna, T. M. (Eds.). (2002). *Large scale assessment programs for all students: Validity, technical adequacy and implementation.* Mahwah, NJ: Lawrence Erlbaum Associates.

Tobin, T. (2005). *Archival records.* In M. Hersen, G. Sugai, & R. Horner (Eds.), *Encyclopedia of behavior modification and cognitive behavior therapy: Vol. 3* (pp. 1143–1147). Thousand Oaks, CA: Sage Publications.

Tobin, T. (2006). *Positive behavior support systems: Value added from use of School Wide Information System.* Eugene: University of Oregon, College of Education. Retrieved November 5, 2008, from http://uoregon.edu/~ttobin/positive2.pdf

Van Acker, R., Grant, S. H., & Henry, D. (1996). Teacher and student behavior as a function of risk for aggression. *Education and Treatment of Children, 19,* 316–334.

VanDerHeyden, A. M. (2005). Prompting. In M. Hersen, G. Sugai, & R. Horner (Eds.), *Encyclopedia of behavior modification and cognitive behavior therapy: Vol. 3* (pp. 1470–1471). Thousand Oaks, CA: Sage Publications.

Walker, H., Colvin, G., & Ramsey, E. (1995). *Antisocial behavior in school: Strategies and best practices.* Pacific Grove, CA: Brooks/Cole.

Walker, H. M., & Rankin, R. (1983). Assessing the behavioral expectations and demands of less restrictive setting. *School Psychology Review, 1,* 274–284.

Walker, H. M., & Walker, J. E. (1991). *Coping with noncompliance in the classroom: A positive approach for teachers.* Austin, TX: Pro-Ed.

Wolery, M. (2005). Errorless learning. In M. Hersen, G. Sugai, & R. Horner (Eds.), *Encyclopedia of behavior modification and cognitive behavior therapy: Vol. 3* (pp. 1296–1299). Thousand Oaks, CA: Sage Publications.

Young, K. R., West, R. P., Smith D. J., & Morgan, D. P. (1991). *Teaching self-management strategies to adolescents.* Longmont, CO: Sopris West Educational Services.

Index

CORWIN
A SAGE Company

The Corwin logo—a raven striding across an open book—represents the union of courage and learning. Corwin is committed to improving education for all learners by publishing books and other professional development resources for those serving the field of PreK–12 education. By providing practical, hands-on materials, Corwin continues to carry out the promise of its motto: **"Helping Educators Do Their Work Better."**